DIARY OF A DOG PATCHER

Diary of a Dog Patcher

a memoir

Casey Carpenter

Cover design by David Ter-Avanesyan
Edited by Joie Davidow

ISBN (paperback): 979-8-9992469-0-5
ISBN (ebook): 979-8-9992469-5-0
Printed in the United States of America

First Edition

For more information,
visit: https://patcherpress.com

DEDICATION: TO MY CHILDREN

To my stepdaughter, **London Perry**—
Baby girl, you've inspired me since you
were just eleven years old. You have a
strength I admire, an attitude I envy, and a
beauty — inside and out — that makes me
so proud of the woman you've become.

I love you forever.

To my daughter, **Ciera Donthnier**
Sis, I've loved you since the moment I found
out I was pregnant with you. Becoming your
mother changed everything about my mission
to overcome grief. If it weren't for you, I truly
don't think I would have made it. I love you
deeply, and I'm so proud to be your mom.

To my son, **Max Boston**
Bub, I wish I could peek into your thoughts just
once. Your sweetness, your innocence, your brilliant
smile and joyous laugh make you the brightest
star in my sky. I love you to the moon and back.

You will always be my baby.

ACKNOWLEDGEMENTS

Thank you to my sister, **Amie Payne**, for being part of my test audience as I worked through this memoir. Your enthusiasm is contagious, and I love being part of your family.

Thank you to my best friend, **Jennifer Judd,** for having my back every step of the way. I love you like a sister, and I always will.

And to **The Avett Brothers** — Your music found me when I couldn't find myself. You held space for sorrow and joy, for ache and hope. You didn't just write songs — you wrote survival. This story doesn't tell that part yet. But it exists because your music walked me through the dark. Thank you for the light.

PROLOGUE

I was parked in the driveway. Max was napping in the backseat, and I was behind the wheel crying, wondering how I'd lost myself so completely. I'd set out to survive. To make sense of the ache in my chest that never quite left. To untangle the inherited grief, I'd felt even before I had language. To break the cycle of silence before it broke my children.

This story isn't about perfect healing. It's not a self-help manual or a redemption arc with a tidy bow at the end. It's a story of facing hard truths, surviving the impossible, and learning to live with honesty and intention. It's a story of bloodlines and breakdowns. Of resilience forged in silence. Of mistakes I made and truths I almost didn't tell.

It's about a family — my family — who taught me how to hold everything in until it shattered. And how I slowly, painfully, learned to do it differently.

You'll meet them here. Those who shaped me. Loved me. Hurt me. Lost themselves along the way. You'll meet the ghosts I still carry, the living I still fight for, and the children I wrote this for — so they'll know where they come from but not be bound by it.

This is not the version of my life I used to tell people. I used to say things were fine — that I had it under control, that I was just tired, that everything was manageable. It was easier to offer the polished version than to admit how close I was to breaking. This is the version I finally told myself.

If you've ever felt you were born into someone else's unfinished story,

if you've ever loved someone who couldn't stay,

if you've ever wondered whether you could survive what broke you …

this book is for you.

CHAPTER ONE

Carl and Vadie

One lazy Sunday in 2011, I was at Grandma's house on Gladstone Street, drying and putting away the dishes. The smell of supper still lingered in the air and Grandma was a few feet away, lying on the couch in the living room, as she often did.

She'd been watching one of her crime shows, and it was a commercial break. We were talking about simple things — the weather, my schedule for the week, prescriptions that needed to be filled. She wanted to know how Ciera liked school, and I told her I was proud of how well she was doing as a second grader in Miamisburg. When the commercial break ended, we fell quiet.

I emptied my harvest of crumbs from the kitchen tabletop into the trash, and as I leaned over, I saw it.

The hole in the floor.

Evidence of the night more than a decade ago when a shot was fired. How much had changed since then! The house had been filled with voices, laughter, tension, and life. Now it's just Grandma and me, two survivors in a house echoing with memories.

I wondered how much longer she would be with us. After all she'd been through, I was surprised she'd lasted this long. A lifetime flashed before my eyes, and I knew it was time to tell the story. The journey of unraveling my past had begun.

I need to start at the beginning, with my grandparents.

They were the strongest people I've ever known. I've seen them carry caskets, comfort grieving families, and cook Sunday dinner for twelve after burying a child without ever once asking for help. It was a quiet strength, steady, constant, unshakable. A strength that came from surviving, enduring one heartbreaking loss after another. Losing a loved one changes you. Losing many reshapes your soul.

By the time Grandma died in 2012, ten days before her ninetieth birthday, she had buried her parents, all six siblings, her husband of more than fifty years, and five of the six children she raised. I'm the last child left.

Some days, that feels heavier than it sounds.

I have firsthand evidence of their grief. They raised

me from the time I was born. I grew up attending the funerals of loved ones — aunts, uncles, family friends. Someone was always dying, but my grandparents never let on that they were sad.

I almost never saw Grandma cry. We just got dressed up like we were headed to church and went to say our goodbyes. That was how we coped. We followed the family rules and showed up without ever discussing anything uncomfortable.

The daughter of Daniel and Annie Back, Grandma was born on January 12, 1922, in rural southeastern Kentucky, and raised in a wooden shack on a small farm along Quicksand Creek. They named her Vada Lee, but everyone called her Vadie. She and her six siblings attended a one-room schoolhouse and the Southern Baptist Church was a central part of their lives.

Vadie had a way with animals. Her mule, Sam, occasionally let her ride him, and her job was to tend the family's chickens, milk the cows, and care for whatever else they had — maybe a pig, or a goat or two. Life was so lean, the children sometimes went days without food. Store-bought clothes and shoes were rare luxuries. Grandma told stories of digging wild onions from the field and eating them raw when there was nothing else, like *Little House on the Prairie* but harder.

She worked on the farm and attended school until she married a local boy named Herman Stamper and gave birth to a daughter, Phyllis, when she was just seventeen. The war came, and Herman left Grandma and the baby for another woman.

Grandma was never open when I would ask her about that marriage. She just said, "He cheated on me."

After the war, Carl Carpenter, a sharp-looking soldier she knew from Quicksand Creek, made it back home to Kentucky. Vadie was on her own, and he began to court her. Carl was one of the eight offspring of Sewell and Callie Carpenter, so his background was as humble as hers had been.

On April 20, 1946, they were married by a Justice of the Peace in Dayton, Ohio and moved into a small house on Grant Street in Old North Dayton where they raised three children: Randall, born in November 1947; Vivian Ann, born in December 1951; and my mom, Carla Sheryl, born in May 1955.

In the spring of 1966, they moved into a house they'd built on Gladstone Street in Moraine, Ohio. They'd bought a double corner lot in what would come to be known as "Dog Patch," a quaint neighborhood of single-family houses on three streets, Gladstone being in the middle. It had its own elementary school, Moraine Meadows; a Southern Baptist church,

Moraine City Baptist; a corner candy store, Mitchell's; and a cluttered craft supply shop named Cappel's — like Hobby Lobby, but more chaotic and, somehow, more charming.

As a kid, I'd go in there and stare longingly at the doll furniture. I wanted one of those fancy dollhouses — the kind with working lights, tiny framed pictures on the walls, and little rugs.

My grandparents had grown up farming the hills of Breathitt County, Kentucky. They'd lived through the Depression and World War II and didn't come from money. They'd worked harder than most for everything they had and earned every cent.

So, they held on to their money tightly and didn't spend it on what they considered wasteful things — like toys or fancy treats for the kids. But in their thrift, they gave us something priceless — a sense of resilience, of knowing how to do without and carry on. It shaped the way I view security, sacrifice, and what it means to truly provide.

Grandpa had a good steady income from his job with Frigidaire. By the late 1960s, Phyllis and Randall had grown up and married but my grandparents opened their doors to nieces and nephews who had lost their parents. They took care of Mom, Aunt Viv, and my cousins Verna, Pam, and Daniel when they needed a place to stay. They were all still in school, and Grandma took them in without hesitation. The Carpenters were blessed with enough funds that she didn't have to work outside the home.

I often imagine how life was for her when all her children were alive and safe — two kids off on their own and two more well on their way in school. I like to think they were a typical American family of the late '60s and early '70s. I wonder if Grandma and Grandpa hugged and kissed each other back then. I rarely saw that. They didn't argue much, but they weren't affectionate in front of others.

They showed their love by being there for each other every step of the way, a united front against the sorrow thrust upon them, supporting each other through the difficulties life threw their way. I'm speculating — I never heard them discuss how they were doing, but it must have been hard.

When I was four years old, Grandpa survived open heart surgery and retired with full benefits. I watched Grandma change the dressing on his chest as she sat on the edge of the bed. It was infected and made her gag to change the dressings, but she did it anyway. She was always caring for someone.

We had a house and cars and stuff, so I thought we were well enough off. Friends and family had less than we did. My grandparents gave me the happiest childhood they could. We each got a gift at Christmas and usually one for our birthdays, but that was it. I didn't get most of the things I wanted. I wore my brother's hand-me-downs and rarely got new clothes.

Because my friends had cool clothes and toys, I felt different, as though I was watching the other kids live the life I couldn't have.

Grandma and Grandpa spent their retirement years raising us and loved my brother and me like their own. Hell, they loved every child who crossed their doorway. They did their best to give us all a good life, taught us right from wrong, and sent us to church.

Hugs and kisses were sparingly bestowed. We rarely heard, "I love you." It just wasn't their way. Instead, they showed us love by teaching us. Grandpa taught us how to use tools and work with things that need fixing. Grandma taught me how to cook and clean. Her job was caring for the house and family, and she was damn good at it.

She drank beer and smoked cigarettes while she was cooking, and I prayed the cigarette ash didn't land in the food. We kids made fun of her for it.

Grandpa was always in the yard or the garage, tinkering around, building and repairing things. He was a skilled carpenter who made the porch furniture. He knew how to work on cars and handed down his skills to my older brother, Kelly. During high school, Kelly spent many an hour in the garage, rebuilding engines or making modifications to whichever project he had that week.

It's hard to think about Kelly when he was still so lively, before the downward spiral that took his young life. Grandma loved Kelly like a son, and it broke her heart to know that his life was filled with pain. He had wit and humor and could make you laugh so hard you'd cry, but he was also clinically depressed and wrestled with demons every day.

I saw what watching him struggle did to Grandma, but she never said a word about the guilt or fear. She just cooked and cleaned and kept going. That was her way.

Grandma and Grandpa never talked about how loss and grief affected them. Their first child, Viv, was killed at the age of eighteen in a car accident. The police came to their door at ten that night to tell them their daughter wouldn't be coming home … ever.

I believe their foundation crumbled when they lost her. They turned to alcohol to numb the pain, drinking beer, wine or liquor every day. At times, I was afraid, not knowing how drunk they were or if I could approach them. Most of the time, I tiptoed around and avoided them as much as possible because their moods were so unpredictable.

Not long after I moved out, they stopped drinking. Grandma even gave up cigarettes. They outlived their need for alcohol but passed it down to my mother and brother. I'm sure Grandma and Grandpa quit drinking when they saw what alcohol was doing to Kelly.

After they lost Viv, they were blessed with two grandchildren — my brother and me. I can only imagine how they must have felt when new life came into their home so soon. It was surely a distraction from the pain.

In June 1990, during the week before my high school graduation, my Aunt Phyllis died after a long battle with lung cancer. She'd been Grandma's first-born child, a strong and beautiful soul who loved God and her family.

We cancelled my graduation party. I felt the loss, but Grandma bore the weight of it internally without sharing her feelings. She kept the devastation of burying another child inside.

Then Grandpa passed, and it was like a piece of her left with him. She got quieter. Slower. More tired. We hired my best friend's older sister to help with the chores. Jamie was a perfect fit and worked for our family for many years, cleaning, running errands, helping with odd jobs, and keeping Grandma company. I'm so grateful we had her because she made it possible for Grandma to stay in her own home until the end.

Grandpa passed in 2004, the week after Thanksgiving, and just after his 89th birthday. Grandma survived him for another seven years. Toward the end, I became her caregiver, stopping in daily to fix her breakfast and organize her meds.

I was frequently assisted by family and close family friends. My cousin Verna was often around when things were bad. She'd helped with my mom, my grandpa, and my grandma in their times of need. I wasn't alone, but the bulk of Grandma's everyday care fell on me. I wouldn't change that. It was an honor and a privilege to help someone who had given so freely of herself. Grandma was a kind of woman who showed up, gave what she had, and asked for nothing in return. We were all better for her love.

But she had a mean streak.

She had a switch that could flip without warning. One moment, she'd be frying bacon and humming an old hymn, and the next she'd snap with a fury that left us stunned.

Discipline came from the peach tree in the backyard. It never bore fruit, but it gave generously in other ways. Its thin, flexible branches were cut down and stripped bare, and Grandma used them across our legs. Sometimes our arms. Sometimes our backs. No explanation. No lesson. Just pain and then silence. And life went on like nothing had happened.

That was how kids were handled at the time. I'm not excusing it. That's just the way it was. You could be laughing one minute and bruised the next, and nobody asked questions.

Still, Grandma was a loving woman who stepped in when others stepped out. She mothered more than her own children and did the best she could with what she had — despite the grief, rage, and the funerals she carried behind her eyes. She was my hero when I was little, always there no matter what was happening. Cooking breakfast. Getting us off to school. Enduring our teenage moods and Kelly's long, stormy seasons of defiance. She showed up every day with the same quiet devotion. I see now that she was more sullen than angry. The grief she carried like a second skin softened her at the edges, even when her words stayed sharp.

I believe she's reunited with her children now, with her husband and the family she buried piece by piece over a lifetime. That faith carries me. It keeps me putting one foot in front of the other. I know I'll see them again, and I want to meet them with a healed heart, a life made whole, and I don't want my children to carry the weight I did.

Grandma and Grandpa taught me what strength looks like — even when it hurts. Now I'm learning what healing looks like, and I want to pass that on. My grandparents were a glowing example of love through survival. I want to be an example of love through transformation. This is where that work begins.

That evening, I tossed the crumbs in the trash and looked at her lying on the couch, her eyes closed now. Breathing slowly. The TV crime show had faded into the background. The hole in the kitchen floor wasn't just a scar in the linoleum, it was a marker of all we'd survived. Of everything that happened in this house but somehow didn't kill us. I wiped my hands on a dish towel and stood still for a moment, letting it settle. The silence. The weight. The call to begin.

CHAPTER TWO

Viv

Vivian Ann was Grandma's second daughter, her third child, and the first to break her heart. She was the ghost we couldn't talk about. The name we dared not mention.

After my grandparents died, I inherited the bright blue chest that had lived in the back bedroom closet for as long as I could remember. It had been off-limits. Mysterious. Vivian's.

Aunt Viv was a name, a story, a photograph, the first verse of the family anthem: "Don't Talk About Uncomfortable Things." Death is uncomfortable. It might upset someone. Early on, we learned not to voice our emotions.

I've come to learn that Aunt Viv was much more than a photograph. She was a good student with beautiful penmanship who loved art, especially working with clay. She was known for her curiosity and creativity, often sketching cartoons in the margins of her notebooks.

Her teachers admired her attention to detail. Her friends said she could always make them laugh, even on their worst days.

My cousin Verna recently shared a memory. She and Viv had been riding a bicycle back from Moraine Meadows, Viv at the handlebars, Verna perched up front, when Verna's foot slipped into the bike spokes. The bike flipped, launching them onto the pavement. "My white oxfords saved my foot for sure," Verna wrote. "Viv was laughing the whole way down." I can picture those two wild girls, scraped knees and all, laughing like hell, because that's what you did when you were young and free and full of nerve.

Viv was blonde and blue-eyed, scrappy and sharp, a girl who could win a debate, outrun the boys, and walk away with her nails still perfect. She and her crew — Pam, Fonda, and Wanda —wore Levi jackets and ran like a pack. Fairmont West eventually banned the jackets, claiming they looked too much like a gang. That was Viv. Defiant. Electric. Unapologetically herself. The kind of girl who stomped another girl with her skates at the Germantown rink and never bothered to apologize. Not because she was cruel, but because she didn't believe in backing down.

She died in March 1970 at the age of eighteen, a senior in high school, weeks from graduation. The driver lost control. The crash was brutal. The injuries were catastrophic.

It cracked the Carpenter family wide open.

They didn't have the tools — no therapy, no support groups, no language for trauma. Just beer. Liquor. Silence. In our family, grief didn't get named. It got buried. And it stayed buried, until it turned into something else.

Just after the funeral, Grandpa took Viv's older brother, Randall, to her grave at Woodland Cemetery. They drank. They cried. They collapsed into the grass, swallowed by sorrow. I wasn't there, but I know that moment broke something in them both.

I don't think anyone in our family ever fully came back from losing her.

Sometimes, I imagine that Viv and I would have been fast friends. She would have been the "cool" aunt, sneaking me sips of wine, helping me forge notes to skip school, taking me to the movies on a Wednesday just because. I wonder if she would've been there in the hard seasons — beside me during Max's hospital stays, holding space when I broke. Maybe she would have been the steady hand my mom needed, too. A confidante. A soft place to land.

Carla never talked to me about how Viv's death affected her, but I know it changed everything. She was only fourteen when her sister died. That kind of loss rewires you. In many ways, it rewired all of us. The silence around Viv's death became part of our family dynamic. It taught me early that you carried grief quietly. You didn't share it. That silence shaped the distance between my mother and me.

When Viv died, something in our family broke apart and was never patched together.

I'm trying. One memory, one story, one truth at a time.

Viv's trunk lives in my home — scuffed, heavy, humming with her presence. Sometimes I open it and imagine what she would have become. I wonder if the doll with the wardrobe is still in there, little dresses on tiny hangers lined up in perfect rows. Verna said it was the coolest doll she'd ever seen. That's how I like to remember Viv, somewhere between girlhood and womanhood, still holding her doll and wearing that gang jacket like armor.

She never got to finish her story.

But I will.

CHAPTER THREE

Phyllis

Phyllis Laverne was Grandma's child from her first marriage. To me, she was the epitome of strength and character. She had the prettiest hands I'd ever seen — long fingers, perfect cuticles, and nails always done in rich, feminine tones. When I was about seven or eight, she painted my nails. I wanted whatever color she was wearing. Her scent was a blend of cigarettes and a sweet floral perfume. Even now, that scent brings her back to me.

To my young eyes, her makeup made her look like a movie star — all eyeliner and elegance. Her beauty was calm, not loud or flashy, but steady. Like someone who could apply eyeliner with a steady hand in a hurricane.

But she had a strictness about her, especially with her kids — Ki, Scott, and Kendra— who were a bit older than Kelly and me. We loved visiting our cousins at their home in Huber Heights.

In Kendra's bedroom, soft light filtered through the window and we played under the tree in the backyard like it was a portal to another world. Uncle Bill and Aunt Phyllis always made us feel welcome, part of something whole and warm.

Even when she snapped at the kids or enforced her rules, there was something admirable about the way she carried herself. I could tell she had standards — for her home, for her family, for herself. And I respected that.

In the late summer of 1987, at the age of fifteen, I landed in the emergency room after a family reunion at Sycamore Trails Park. My side ached so badly we thought it might be appendicitis. But it was a grapefruit-sized cyst on my right ovary. Emergency surgery followed, and I came out with flying colors.

When Aunt Phyllis came to visit me, she didn't fuss. She didn't baby me. She asked direct questions about the surgery, and when I didn't know the answers, she drew me a diagram of the female reproductive system—ovaries, fallopian tubes, uterus— and explained exactly what they'd taken out. No sugar-coating. No weirdness. Just facts delivered with care and clarity. That moment left a mark. She'd respected me enough to tell me the truth — and in doing so, taught me something about being a woman.

Later, cancer shrunk her body, stole her curves, dulled her once-bold laugh. When I saw her in that hospital bed, quiet and hollowed out, I felt I was watching a lighthouse go dim. The perfume was gone. The lipstick. The brightness. But even in that state, she kept her dignity. There was still something regal about her — even in a hospital gown, even in pain.

When the Lord finally took her, I told myself she'd earned her rest, endured enough. But that didn't stop the ache. Some losses don't scream; they hum. Quiet and constant.

We weren't the closest. Not in the way some people are with their aunts. But she mattered to me. She left fingerprints on my girlhood — in the way I shaped my own sense of beauty, asked questions when things didn't make sense, the way I try to carry myself with composure, even in chaos.

She was one of the first women I admired. And I still do. I still like to paint my nails and wear makeup when I go out, even if things aren't so bright on the inside.

CHAPTER FOUR

Randall

I thought Uncle Randall was a troublemaker turned lonely, the polar opposite of Aunt Phyllis. She was good and he was bad. Randall cussed and drank and smoked like a party animal, while Phyllis went to church and was always cleaned up and pretty. They were yin and yang. Opposites in every way, but they both showed me something about survival — one through grace, the other through grit.

Uncle Randall scared me a little, not in a monster-under-the-bed way, but in a real-life-wild-card way. I never knew if he was going to hug me or holler at me. His energy could fill a room. He was fast-talking, always moving, drink in hand, jokes flying. But I thought that beneath all that noise, he was lonely. Maybe even broken.

He and my Aunt Kathy had two children, Brandon and Nicholas. While they were waiting for their new house to be built, they moved in with us, and we became more like siblings than first cousins.

It was a beautiful custom home in West Alexandria on Twin Creek, if I remember correctly. I don't know how long they stayed with us, but to my four- or five-year-old self, it felt like a lifetime. I remember having to wait for the bathroom, and the feeling that too many people were under one roof. It was cramped, for sure.

Not long after they settled into their dream house, Randall and Kathy divorced, and I felt sorry for Brandon and Nicholas. Randall got married again to a woman named Pam, but that didn't last, either — loud fights, slammed doors, and more than one night that ended in police threats and bruises.

One Thanksgiving, we were all sitting down to eat — me, Grandma, Grandpa, Mom, Randall, Pam, Kelly, and I think Brandon and Nick. I don't know what happened before dinner, but Randall and Pam were into it. Screaming turned to crashing — plates flying, chairs shifting, the whole dinner upset.

Grandma threatened to call the police. Grandpa took his plate into the living room and kept eating. Eventually, Randall and Pam straightened up and the dinner settled back down. As usual, we acted like nothing had happened and went on with our day.

Growing up, I struggled to respect Uncle Randall. He always seemed a little unhinged, as though his engine was running hot but nobody was at the wheel. He drank and did drugs — coke, I'd bet — and was always a source of turmoil. But Grandma thought he walked on water. He was a mommy's boy, for certain.

While he was still working, I did his taxes, and we grew rather fond of each other. I think he was proud of me for having worked my way through college and landing stable employment. I know he appreciated my help. He always paid me more than he should have.

In the mid-2000s, a few years after Grandpa died, I drove down to Kentucky to spend an afternoon with Randall and Grandma at the family farm. Randall was a gracious host — kind, attentive, calm. He didn't seem drunk or high that day, which was a nice change.

We talked for hours. He asked thoughtful questions. He listened. It was one of the only times I saw him as simply a man — not the wildcard, not the trouble-maker, just Randall. For a little while, the chaos fell away, and I glimpsed a softness in him I'll never forget.

By the time he retired, he was separated from Pam and moved to the family farm on Quicksand Creek. I was glad he was there to care for the land where our roots were planted. That home meant the world to my grandparents.

I'll never forget summers there, playing outside with Kelly, roaming the hills. Part of me still lives there, and although the house is no longer livable, I long to return.

Randall cared for the property as Grandpa would have. When a neighbor tried to claim part of our land as his own, he protected it. After months of filing complaints with the local police and trading angry words with the neighbor, it came to a head.

In August in 2009, Randall was mowing the grass when the neighbor drove down the long driveway, stopped his car, and pulled a gun from the trunk. Randall often carried his own weapon for protection from wildlife while mowing.

A shootout began.

The neighbor shot first. Randall fired back, hitting the man twice. The neighbor survived with no life-threatening injuries, but a bullet found its way into Randall's brain and he died that day at the end of the driveway, protecting his birthright, defending the sacred land of our ancestors, the place that held our memories, our summers, and our ghosts. He was wild and reckless, but he died with a purpose.

I still see him in dreams, standing tall in the fields,

unbothered by the chaos that once defined him. Maybe that's how I'll choose to remember him, not for the Thanksgiving fights or drunken stumbles, but as a man who, for all his flaws, guarded our past.

That land carried the echoes of so many others before him, especially my mother who was born into that legacy in that house, that silence, the weight of grief that would eventually shape and shatter, her life.

CHAPTER FIVE

Carla

Carla, my mother, was my grandparents' last child, born on May 27, 1955. She was Daddy's girl and a bit spoiled, but beautiful inside and out. She loved horses, and when she was little, they bought her one.

The youngest of four children — four years younger than her sister, Viv — she grew up happy. I'd like to think she and Viv were great friends, but Mom was probably a pain in the ass, too young to hang out. I'm sure she was a handful. When she was in school, they nicknamed her "Bug." Some of her old friends still call her that. Uncle Randall said it was because she was always bugging him.

Because of their age difference, I don't imagine Mom and Uncle Randall had much of a relationship. I think she and Viv shared a room, so it had to be earth-shattering to lose her sister so tragically, even if they got on each other's nerves.

It should come as no surprise that she got pregnant with my older brother three months after her sister's death. She must have been in shock, consumed by grief, and looking for the love she wasn't receiving from her parents who were mourning so deeply, they were numbing themselves. That's what I saw when I was old enough to make memories.

There was always an air of sadness in our house. Sometimes it was so thick, it woke me up, especially during the rare nights when I heard Grandma crying.

One night, Grandma got really drunk and fell asleep on the couch. I heard loud snoring and came out to check on her. She must have been dreaming. She woke up and told me Phyllis was coming to get us, and I had to sit there with her until she arrived.

Even at that age, I knew Phyllis wasn't coming. It was the middle of the night, and Grandma was too drunk to know what she was saying. But I had to sit there in my little rocking chair, in the dark, wearing my nightgown while I waited for an aunt who wasn't coming. When Grandma passed out again, I went back to bed. I was scared and angry. I never checked on Grandma again, I just lay awake in my bed and hoped she'd go to bed on her own. Sometimes she did, sometimes she didn't.

I don't know if my mother noticed that her parents had drinking issues, but I know she liked to party. Her favorites were Miller Lite and Tequila. She also smoked pot, and, for a time, grew and sold weed. She took prescription medicine for depression and anxiety. I'm sure she was told she couldn't drink on those meds, but she was not one to listen to instructions. She was bull-headed and stood her ground. Like Grandma, she had a mean streak and a good heart.

She was our mother, but she was never ours the way we needed her to be. If I'm going to tell this story honestly, I'll have to start with the part that's hardest to admit.

She left us long before she died.

In my first memory of her, I'm four years old and she's picking me and Kelly up for a sleepover. At the time, she was living in an apartment with her boyfriend. We were so excited to see Mom. I packed a little overnight bag and wore my favorite red coat with a faux fur collar and cuffs that made me feel warm and fancy like a princess.

When we got to the apartment, I struggled with the

buttons, but nobody offered to help me. By the time I got the coat off, I was so frustrated, I threw it on the ground. No one noticed. If they had, they would have seen that it landed on the space heater.

The next day when it was time to leave, there were burn marks on the coat. Even the fancy fur was singed. I was devastated but didn't want to show it, so, my response was silence. I was alone with my thoughts, telling myself it wasn't important. She wasn't the mom I needed.

That night after dinner, I went to the bathroom. When I was finished, I called Mom to come wipe me, as I was used to doing with Grandma. I don't remember her exact words, but it was something like, "I don't wipe asses. Figure it out yourself!" Horrified, I cleaned myself up. I was so embarrassed, I felt like crying. How was I supposed to know I should have been wiping my own butt?

Carla was still in her teens when she had my brother Kelly and me. Our dad wasn't really in the picture. He was just too wild, too crazy, too free, and Grandma and Grandpa were angry with him. Carla wasn't prepared to be a mother. She lived in and out of her parents' house. Sometimes, she'd be gone for days, sometimes longer. I believe that she loved us but just couldn't stay.

Eventually, she stopped trying.

When I was five, and Kelly was six, our grandparents decided to formally adopt us. Carla signed the papers and relinquished whatever fragile hope she still had of being our mom.

She moved out of the house and into a life shaped by battered love, bottles, and blame. But she never disappeared entirely. She drifted around the edges of our lives, sometimes showing up with gifts or promises, sometimes calling out of the blue, sometimes not calling at all. She lived with boyfriends and friends. She smoked too much and drank even more. She moved from place to place and job to job like a woman trying to outrun her own shadow.

Even when she wasn't around, she was there — in our habits, our anger, our wondering why she couldn't stay.

I know I must've seen her when I was five, because there's a photo of us holding hands at Christmas 1977. But I don't remember it.

I remember that at the age of six, I'd lie in bed, staring at the hallway shadows. The number "7" appeared, outlined by the door frame and light. And I thought, *Next time it's my birthday; I'll be seven.* Funny, the memories we hold onto and those we let go.

That year, I woke up to shouting and flashing red and blue lights bleeding through my curtains. I stood up in bed and looked out the window. The Moraine police were slamming Mom against the trunk of her car and trying to cuff her, but she was fighting them tooth and nail, screaming and yelling.

They shoved her face down and body pinned her. Even at the age of six, I could tell they weren't trying to calm her down. They were trying to break her, and I wondered what she'd done that was so bad.

I screamed for them to stop. Kelly ran in and we helplessly watched together, yelling and crying at the horror movie unrolling before us. He looked confused, scared, older than his years.

We saw Grandma and Grandpa come out and try to talk to the cops. Then Grandma came back in and pulled us away from the window. She told us to go back to bed. No explanation. No comfort.

I didn't tell anybody until I was much older and the details were etched into my brain. Not once did Kelly or I talk with our grandparents about the horror of that night. Not once did we talk about the drinking and the drugs and the violence. It wasn't how we did things. The next morning, we got up and kept moving as though nothing had happened.

I need to break that cycle of silence. It leaves me alone, trying to work through it all with nothing but my imagination.

When I was twelve, Mom got in a fight with her boyfriend, and my grandfather went to get her. I'm not sure why my brother and I came with him. She'd walked two and half miles from her home to the Dayton Mall. I remember thinking that she must really have wanted to get away. She was beaten and bruised, her face red and swollen. We took her to the hospital, where they found a broken finger — minor in the scheme of things. I remembered that she'd been treated for broken ribs once before. She stayed with us a few nights, then went back.

I don't know how many beatings she took while she lived with that man, but I'm aware of something like five or six events. At the time, I only saw her occasionally, so I am not sure what her life was like. I can only imagine that she must have lived in constant fear. Now that I'm an adult, I so wish I could talk to her.

We had good times after that. When I was fourteen and fifteen, during the summer she'd let me stay for a few nights at a time at the house where she lived with her boyfriend. She had horses and chickens and a pond, and we'd do the morning feeds together. Then she'd make me breakfast — her famous double decker, extra pickle, delicious BLT. I don't know why those sandwiches tasted so much better when she made them.

On my sixteenth birthday, I invited a few friends to her place, and we had a great time, until I noticed that Mom was missing. When she finally emerged, her eyes were red from crying, and she was holding an ice pack against her face. Later, she showed me that'd he knocked a back tooth out. He'd hit her that hard.

She kept trying to play hostess as though nothing had happened. I knew the truth, and I ignored it, just like she did.

That suppression of any unpleasantness creates a trauma passed down through generations. Never speak of it. Whatever "it" is.

But I'm speaking now. Because silence didn't save her. And it won't save me.

Once when I was staying with Mom, I had a stomach flu. I was throwing up and all that fun stuff, and she did a great job caring for me, so for a short time, I felt like we had a real mother-daughter relationship. But I always ended up back at Grandma's.

After a few years, she found the strength to leave that boyfriend. She had several relationships after that. Some were physically abusive, some were not.

For several years, Mom was working as a receptionist at Fickert's construction company and did their accounts receivable and billing. When they needed someone to do their accounts payable and payroll, Mom recommended I apply.

I was hired as a full-time clerk. It was an open office, and my desk was next to Mom's. We ate lunch together every day, and she taught me the ropes. I learned to use a radio/dispatch system. I hated it, but she coached and trained me until I got used to it.

I loved working with her. During the day, she was sober. She'd bought a farm in Miamisburg for her horses. At the time my first husband and I had an apartment there, so Mom and I were close both at work and at home. I miss those days so much.

She encouraged me to take accounting classes with her, and even offered to pay my tuition. So, in the fall of 1994, we signed up at Sinclair Community College in Dayton. I stuck with it. She didn't. I can't recall what kept her from taking classes. She worked full-time and had her horses, so it was probably hard for her to prioritize homework. But she inspired me to get started, and I owe my college education to her.

School came easy for me, especially accounting. During my senior year at Fairmont High School, I'd taken an accounting course and I *loved* it. It made sense to me, and I excelled at all things accounting. For years, I worked in the cash office at Drug Emporium and as an assistant store manager. I was still working there when Mom recruited me. She was devastated when I announced I'd taken a job at Brockman and Co., a small local CPA firm. While working in the accounting office to get my foot in the door, I could continue to take classes and maybe go on to become a CPA.

I know she was proud of me but saddened that we'd no longer be working together. It made a break in our relationship. Silly, now that I look back on it.

I went on to secure a position at Brockman & Co. and, in the spring of 1999, I earned an associate's degree in accounting from Sinclair.

We had a big party to celebrate, and Mom showed up to help with the food. We had a keg of beer in the garage and set up the backyard with chairs and music. It was the biggest party I remember at that house.

Mom began drinking from the keg early. Eventually, she just parked herself beside it. I was busy attending to friends and sneaking off to smoke cigarettes – a nasty habit I hid from my grandparents for years because they would have been disappointed if they found out. They must have known, though. I must have smelled of cigarettes.

Again, anything even a little awkward was never discussed. We'd all pretend it wasn't there and behave like it never happened. But it bubbled out in other ways. I was taught by example to numb those feelings with drink and postpone worrying about my demons.

At that party, Mom got too drunk too early and was loud and obnoxious. While she was babysitting the keg in the garage, she decided to show off a bud from her latest harvest.

She had a large Tupperware container filled with nugs and was rolling a joint when my boss from the CPA firm arrived. I hesitated to invite him in because Mom was showing her ass.

I believe mental health disorders were a part of my past going back to my mom and I could see signs in Uncle Randall, as well. Aunt Phyllis was also a very nervous person when she was around us. She chain smoked, and her hands shook all the time. I remember noticing how fidgety she was while she was painting my nails.

Grandma didn't create the 'stuff it down' approach to life, but she damn-near perfected it. I believe many families have secrets. In those days, people didn't talk much about feelings. Grandma inherited the pattern of avoiding difficult conversations and passed down to both me and my daughter, Ciera, but we're both medicated, and we're not afraid to share our feelings. At least with each other.

By the late '90s Mom had settled down with a man

named Stanley Bristow who seemed to treat her right. They both enjoyed riding horses and motorcycles and got along well. They lived together on her farm in Miamisburg and on November 19, 1999, they were married by the mayor. They seemed to live a happy life.

After we lost my brother Kelly in December 2002, Mom and I became distant, and for a long time, things between us were difficult. When they improved, I hired her to be my daughter's caregiver. She drove the backroads from Miamisburg to the house where my husband and I lived in Union, Ohio and stayed with Ciera until Travis got home from work.

For a few months, it worked well, then she started calling off with no notice, so I couldn't rely on her. I think she was drinking heavily. We had to send Ciera to daycare when she was just nine months old. Oh, how I wish I could have had honest conversations with my mom about hard topics. Maybe then she would have listened and been a more responsible adult. But that's not how it went. I try to tell myself to let go. I can't undo the past.

Shortly before Mom started going downhill, her husband, Stan, joined a motorcycle club and was hanging out with bad people who introduced him to IV drugs. Mom was desperate for him to stop, because until then, the marriage had been going so well.

It devastated her that he was using, and she confided in me regularly about the turmoil in their relationship. She was drinking and popping pills, but she couldn't tolerate IV drug abuse.

On Thanksgiving weekend 2004, Stan came home high. She started a fight and threw things at him. He overpowered her and beat her. By the time he left, her eyes were swollen shut and she had to feel the buttons on the phone to call 911. She survived that beating, and, for once, decided to press charges.

That September, Grandpa had been diagnosed with cancer. Just a few days after Thanksgiving, in the first week of December, he passed.

While she was healing from the beating, Mom lost her dad. She almost didn't go to his funeral but decided to attend at the last minute. Everybody talked about how battered she looked. The swelling was still there, and she was black and blue from head to toe. Many people asked me what had happened to her. It was one of the most difficult days of my life, grieving the tragic loss of Grandpa while bearing the shame explaining that my mom's husband had done that to her.

It took her months to recover physically. I'm sure she never recovered from the shame and humiliation of attending her father's funeral looking like she did.

Stan lost his job. Mom couldn't pay for horse feed, and things were looking bleak. She decided to file for divorce.

She called an attorney and asked me to go with her. I agreed to take the afternoon off work. The appointment she was given was on her fiftieth birthday, Friday, May 27, 2005 at two in the afternoon. I thought she should have asked for a different day. Nobody wants to spend their birthday filing for divorce, but she was strong-willed and insisted on keeping the appointment.

Ciera was only a year and half old. I dropped her off at daycare, kissed her, and headed to work. Around noon, I decided to check in with Mom and left her a voice mail.

At one, I left work to pick Mom up and take her downtown. I called her again from the car and she answered, slurring her words, barely coherent. She was drunk, crying. She said she couldn't go to the appointment and asked me to go without her.

I explained to her that I couldn't file for divorce on her behalf. She'd have to do it herself. We agreed to reschedule the meeting and meet at Grandma's for birthday cake and ice cream that afternoon at 5:30.

I contemplated picking up Ciera from daycare but decided to enjoy the rare time off and went home for a nap instead. I turned off the ringer on my phone and dozed. When Travis got home from work, I lazily picked Ciera up at daycare. I noticed that I'd missed call from my mom. She'd left a message, but I decided to call her back without listening to it. No one answered, and I went home to dress for the party.

I found a stranger there. A young gentleman was going over paperwork with Travis. I got Ciera settled with a snack, then joined the two men in the kitchen. They were discussing the installation of a new home alarm system. Travis and I had talked about it, and the young boy happened to randomly knock on our door that afternoon. The price was reasonable, so we decided to proceed, and Travis began to sign the documents.

Then the phone rang.

"Casey!" Grandma cried. "Get down here right now! Your mother is dead."

"What?" I didn't comprehend what she'd told me.

"Get down here right now! She's gone. Your mother is gone."

I said okay and hung up, then turned to Travis and the salesman in shock. When I told them the news, the salesman left quickly.

Travis asked what happened. "I don't know," I said. I thought she must have overdosed on pills. I told him that I'd talked to her a few hours earlier and she'd been shit faced. I grabbed the diaper bag and a few snacks for Ciera, then headed to Grandma's.

A swarm of relatives were gathered in the kitchen. Mom had been expected there that afternoon, but she never showed up. Grandma couldn't get an answer on my mom's cell or home phone, so she asked her niece, Pam, to check on her.

Pam and her husband Jeff drove out to the farm and saw that her truck was there. They called for her, but she didn't answer. Jeff found her in the barn, lying in a pool of blood with a gun beside her.

They called the police who began investigating it as a homicide but said we'd have to wait for the autopsy results before they could determine the manner of death. They were looking for her husband, Stan. Grandma was convinced she'd been assaulted and began interviewing people who knew her.

She gave to the police every lead she came across. Mom had a violent past, and Grandma was sure an ex-boyfriend had snuck up on her and shot her in the forehead. It was that detail that made the police think it was a homicide.

No one had seen Stan since before her death, but a man from his bike club found me and asked if they could attend her funeral wearing their colors. I said it might be too upsetting for my grandma. Stan never showed.

We held the funeral before the autopsy results came back. Pastor Bill Stanley officiated, and there was a large outpouring of friends and family. The flowers were overwhelming. Travis commented, "Biggest turnout, yet," comparing Mom's funeral to Kelly's and Grandpa's.

I took home a plethora of plants, fresh cut flowers, floral blankets, windchimes, and beautiful gifts. Over the next few days, I grew weary of their scent. What once was a lovely smell became a vivid reminder of funerals, funeral homes, death and grief. To this day, I don't like the smell of fresh flowers.

A few days after her funeral, Stan phoned, and I urged him to turn himself in. He swore he had nothing to do with her death.

After a thorough investigation, it was determined that Stan couldn't have been at Mom's barn that day, because they had him on video in Middletown at the time of death.

A few weeks later, the autopsy results ruled death by suicide.

Grandma didn't want to believe it. I think she secretly hoped it was a homicide, so she wouldn't feel responsible.

When I listened to the voice mail my mom left that day, her last words to me were, "Case. Call me back soon, or it might be too late."

And she'd scribbled on the back of an envelope, "Take care of my horses. I want Ciera to have them. Now I lay me down to sleep."

That day, something shattered in me, but something else broke open. I stopped pretending, stopped playing along with the silence that had protected nothing and no one.

My mother's death didn't just end her story. It demanded that I start telling mine. I couldn't save her, but maybe by telling the truth — the whole truth — I could save us.

The truth is that she was diagnosed with bipolar depression and anxiety. When Kelly and I were adopted, she held her parents responsible for "stealing" us from her.

In her thirties, she sought help and was inpatient at a local hospital for a time. But she didn't follow instructions. Instead, she drank and smoked to avoid her pain.

She was desperate and couldn't find another way out.

I just wish I'd answered her call.

I carry her with me still. In my stubbornness. In my fierce love for my children. In the parts of me that refuse to quit, even when the world goes dark. But I carry her differently now — not as a wound I can't stop touching, but as a woman I'm still learning to forgive.

I used to think her story was a warning — what not to become. Now I see it was also a map. Not a path I was meant to follow, but one I had to learn to walk away from.

Carla wasn't just my mother. She was a daughter. A sister. A girl who never had the tools to process her grief. A woman who loved deeply and hurt deeply and tried, in her own broken way, to survive.

I wish she'd made it. I wish she'd stayed. I wish she'd known how much we still needed her. But I also know that every wish I make now is a prayer I live out loud with my own daughter.

The silence stopped with me. And the healing started.

CHAPTER SIX

Vernon

Writing about my father is harder than I thought it would be, not because the memories are all bad, but because they're scattered, slippery, unfinished. He was never a constant in my life, but he left marks all the same. Some tender. Some jagged. Some I still don't know how to name.

Vernon David Adkins was born and raised with ten brothers and sisters in a two-bedroom house on Gladstone Street in Dog Patch next door to the church. Mom's house was less than a block away, so they knew each other, though they were several years apart in age.

I don't know how or when they met, but they had two children together when they were very young, and neither of them was prepared to be a parent.

Mom's mental struggles weren't diagnosed until

she was in her thirties, but I'm sure she needed help long before then. They were both drinkers and drug users and prioritized that in their lives from a very young age.

I don't know why they didn't work out. I only saw them together a few times, so I don't know what they were like as a couple, but they had no foundation to build a family.

I'm sure Dad had his own mental struggles. In my first memory of him, I'm three or four years old. Kelly and I had been allowed to hang out with him for a few hours, and he took us up to Grandma's attic, rolled a joint and lit it up. He sternly told us we wouldn't be allowed to come back if we told Grandma, so we kept it a secret. I thought Dad was the coolest, handsome with long curly hair.

In my next memory, he picked us up in his blue Camaro with his girlfriend, Teresa, and took us to Frisch's where she worked delivering food to customers in their cars, like the drive-in hamburger joints of the '50s.

I had my first vanilla coke with a burger and fries that day. Our grandparents didn't take us out to eat often, so it was a rare treat, and I loved being with Dad. He was funny, charming, and a little dangerous.

I met Teresa's family at their wedding. Her mother made all the bridesmaid dresses, including my junior bridesmaid dress, and I loved it —light blue with sheer white eyelet. I wore a blue slip under it.

Even before she married Dad, Teresa loved Kelly and me as though we were her own. I'm sure she's the main reason I know my dad at all. She must have encouraged him on his rare visits. I owe her more than she ever knew.

When they had children, first Missy, then Amie, I felt lucky to have baby sisters. I'm sure Kelly would have loved a baby brother. He was jealous of those girls because they got to have Dad every day. As we got older, he acknowledged that it made him resentful, that they got a version of Dad we could only imagine. Even if it wasn't perfect, it was something.

When we were teens and could drive ourselves, Kelly and I began to visit Dad. He moved all over the city of Moraine but for much of my teens and twenties, he and his family lived next door to his parents, Grandma and Grandpa Adkins.

There were no rules. He'd let us drink and smoke, and he was an extremely talented musician who could play lead guitar and sing rock and roll like a star. I loved being around the music.

When Kelly and I were still kids, we went to a bar to hear him play, which was awesome. People cheered at the end of each song.

I often spent time together with Teresa in the kitchen, arranged flowers for her or played with the little girls. Kelly was probably busy being Dad's shadow. He and Dad used to drink together. We never knew what was going to happen. On several occasions, they wrestled. We never had to call the police, but we came close.

Dad always had a guitar in his hands and taught both Kelly and my first husband to play. When he was a teenager, Kelly taught me the only three songs I can play on the guitar, and might have been a guitar instructor, but a bad back, spotty work, and addiction got in the way.

He'd drink and play all night, then show up for a blue-collar job he didn't like. The back pain got the best of him, and he became addicted to pain killers. When the doctors began cracking down on prescriptions, he bought pills on the street. And when he couldn't find the pills, he substituted them with heroin.

Before it got to that, we had good times, talking, laughing, drinking and smoking. I learned to sing without dying of embarrassment because he made me sing in front of him.

Without Dad, I would never have done karaoke, and if I'd never done karaoke, I probably wouldn't have my son Max.

Once Dad rode down Gladstone Street on a kid's bicycle to visit Kelly at Grandma's house. Kelly and his date had just pulled up to the curb after having dinner together, when Dad rolled up shirtless, smoking a cigarette. He wanted to show Kelly where he'd shot himself in the leg with a pellet gun. He always knew how to impress! I believe he scared Kelly's date, because he didn't see her again.

On my twenty-fifth birthday, Kelly threw me a surprise party, as I'd done for him. He held it at Dad's house, and it was a great time, a shining moment in my memory — lots of drinking, smoking, and music.

Then the music got quieter. Dad's calls were less frequent, and the light in his eyes dimmed. The bright moments were fewer and farther apart.

Eventually, he put down his guitar for the last time and picked up heroin again. It didn't let him go. He died from an overdose on March 5, 2014.

We held his celebration of life at the Moraine Civic Center, at the north end of Dog Patch, where so many of us played growing up. We laid out a beautiful spread of photos and guitars — pieces of the man he used to be. I took home no flowers that day. I didn't want to smell them in my house.

I used to wonder what it would have been like to grow up with a dad like other kids. A dad who showed up and remembered birthdays. A dad who wasn't broken.

The truth is, I got pieces. A flash of a smile. A car ride with fries and vanilla Coke. A secret rolled in an attic. A name on a birth certificate that once said father "unknown."

Now I carry his name. His blood. Maybe even some of his demons. But I also carry something he never got the chance to know — healing.

I am not the girl he raised. I'm the woman I became as much because of his absence as his presence.

And for that, I choose to carry love. Not because he earned it, but because I deserve it.

My kids will never have to wonder if they were wanted. Or if they mattered. That cycle ends with me.

CHAPTER SEVEN

Kelly

Carla and Vernon's stories ended in blood and silence, lives marked by invisible battles, loud collapses, and unfinished business. But theirs wasn't the only collapse that shaped my world. The grief I carried for my mother and father didn't arrive all at once. It had been seeded years earlier in the face of another loss I never recovered from, the death of my brother, Kelly.

Kelly wasn't just my sibling, he was my other half. We shared the same beginning, the same wound from having been given away, the same desperate hope that maybe, one day, we'd belong.

This is his chapter. And like Mom's and Dad's, it doesn't end the way I want it to.

David Kelly Carpenter was born to Carla Carpenter and Vernon Adkins on March 14, 1971. His entrance into the world was traumatic. He was forcibly pulled from his mother with forceps, which left him with large bruises on either side of his head near his eyes. In his newborn photo, he looks like he'd been in a bar fight — not born but bruised into the world.

He weighed nearly nine pounds, and Mom was a little bitty fifteen year-old girl, so the birth traumatized them both.

I can only imagine those early weeks — the chaos, the exhaustion, the fear. I've been told that Kelly was a fussy baby. I know that, as a child, he suffered from allergies, psoriasis, and chronic ear infections.

His first few months must have been difficult for Mom. She was madly in love with Dad, but he was a playboy, a musician, a long-haired hippie who liked to drink and party. He couldn't have been ready to settle down, much less be a father.

But he couldn't stay away from Mom. He'd sneak in to see her. Once, Grandpa found Dad's sandals outside the bedroom window and was furious. When Kelly was just six months old, Mom became pregnant with me. I can't imagine the conversation when she had to tell her parents that she was pregnant again.

Kelly was an only child for fifteen months before I arrived: tiny, wheezing, and in need of breathing treatments. What a handful! Grandma had lost Viv, and at a time of so much grief, new life might've felt like a blessing — or a burden. Probably a little of both.

Mom had two babies and was trying to complete her schooling at home when she was just a kid herself. She couldn't have handled much of the responsibility. Grandma must have done a lot of the baby-care during those first few years, and Kelly became her boy.

He was spoiled and given little discipline, while my grandparents were always strict with me. I wasn't allowed to stay at friends' houses or even play over for very long. But Kelly could go anywhere with anyone. Our two first cousins, Brandon and Nick, were nearby and we went to their house a lot.

I'm nearly positive Kelly had ADHD. They didn't diagnose it as often then. He got good grades, and his IQ was in the 140s. He was witty, a jokester who made me the butt of most of his pranks.

He was always in trouble at school for talking in class and acting up, happy at the center of attention. I did my best to stay under the radar and mostly succeeded. But Kelly was Kelly. He'd push the envelope, and most of the time, he got his way.

He was so charming, it was hard not to love him, even when he was being an ass. In high school, he had lots of friends and girlfriends. We both worked at the local drug store after school, and when our shifts matched, we rode there together. One of his close friends was Foster. We'd all hang out drinking and partying.

By the time we were seventeen and eighteen, we both had jobs, so when our grandparents went to Kentucky for the summer, we had to stay put. With the house in Dog Patch to ourselves, we had many a good time, doing beer bongs in the garage, playing poker, smoking, and listening to music.

But somewhere along the way, Kelly changed. I think he'd had undiagnosed mental disorders since he was a kid. He had a history of violence, but I didn't really realize it was a problem until I was an adult.

There were early warning signs. When he was three years old, he hit my friend Jennifer on the head with a hammer, and when he was six, he nearly took off our cousin Brandon's head with a sickle. The older he got, the more violent he became — but he turned his violence inward.

Instead of hurting others, he began to hurt himself. He'd cut or pierce himself to let the demons out. The pain of a new tattoo might make him feel better.

Once he heated a brand in the fireplace and seared his thigh with four by six inch initials — DKC — then showed it to me like a prized possession. He said it hurt so much, he nearly passed out.

I don't know what I should have said, but I just muttered, "Dude, get some help." We didn't have the language for pain back then. I didn't know how to say, "You don't have to hurt to feel real." I didn't even know I needed to say it. We weren't a "let's talk about it" family.

For his twenty-fifth birthday, we threw him a surprise party. He was incredibly surprised, and, for a minute, I worried he'd be angry. He started to get a look in his eyes, then softened and began to smile.

When he took off his coat, we saw a quarter-inch circle of missing skin around his left arm, beneath the edge of his short-sleeved shirt. A grotesque open wound. I knew he'd been cutting himself, but what do you say to somebody who believes his body has been invaded by demons?

I don't know why he had so much self-hatred. Maybe he had abandonment issues. He spent most of his twenties self-medicating and drinking away his woes, until he couldn't hold a job. Couldn't meet friends or family for simple get-togethers. All he could do was hole up in his room and drink. Eventually, if he didn't start the day with a six-pack, he got the shakes.

He lived with me for awhile. Kelly crashed on my couch, because I kept my second bedroom-turned-office stuffed with files and clutter. He brought a few belongings — a pillow, his gaming system, headphones, and CDs. It wasn't much, but it was something. He needed out of that house on Gladstone St. after a series of hospital stays for mental health and addiction.

I preferred having him there at that time. I didn't want him to be discharged from the hospital only to go back to the scene of everything — back to Grandma's, back to the bullet hole in the kitchen floor, back to the house that almost killed him.

I told him straight that he couldn't go back there. If he wanted to stay sober — if he wanted a future — he wouldn't find it where the past nearly destroyed him. After a few months, the pull of old habits dragged him back to drinking and back to Grandma's.

Kelly was only fifteen months older, but people assumed I was the older one, maybe because I'd moved out, finished college, held a steady job — or maybe because I was always picking up his pieces.

Kelly had charm, wit, and an infectious energy that made him the life of the party. But beneath it, he battled alcoholism, depression, and mental health diagnoses that he never truly accepted. Most people never saw that side of him. I did. And I often carried it, in the same way that I carried Mom's chaos — sometimes both at the same time. In our family, pain aged you fast.

He was knowingly poisoning himself. By the time he was twenty-five, doctors told him that if he didn't stop drinking immediately, he'd be dead within five years. He made it five and a half.

His downward spiral in life was sad to watch. He worked when he could, went to Sinclair Community College and earned his certificate. It was mailed to the house a few weeks after he passed. A poignant reminder that he had a lot of good in him, and he truly was intelligent. If only he could have dealt with his demons instead of poisoning them.

When the end came, it was quiet, but it echoed through everything.

Kelly showed me how pain can get passed down, how silence becomes a scar. But he also showed me how much light there can be — even in someone who's falling apart. I wish he'd found a way through the pain. I wish he'd stayed long enough to see how much he mattered. He was my brother, my first best friend, my co-conspirator, my other half.

He taught me what grief looks like when it's swallowed whole. And in losing him, I learned that silence never saves anyone.

So now, I speak. I write. I mother differently. I love louder.

I carry him with me — not just the pain, but the light he never fully shared.

For Kelly. For me. For Ciera. For Max.

CHAPTER EIGHT

Mike

Mike Mosley was the beginning of a lot of things. My first crush. My first real love. My first real loss. His house was next door to Moraine Meadows Elementary, and we met on the playground. He was cute, wore a jean jacket. I liked his smile and the way he laughed with his whole face.

We dated in junior high. He was a year younger than I was, but two grades behind me. That embarrassed me a little, and I decided to break up so I could date a high school boy. At the time, it made sense. I was only fourteen and didn't want to be tied down.

In my sophomore year of high school, I had a few boyfriends, and the following year, I began dating my brother's friend Foster, a whirlwind romance that involved a lot of drugs and alcohol. I was high on acid, mushrooms, or weed, and, on weekends, we always had alcohol.

We both worked at Drug Emporium after school. Then Foster quit. And when he broke up with me, I was crushed.

Not long after the breakup with Foster, I ran into Mike again — maybe at a party, maybe around town. When I saw him, I felt like I'd been holding my breath for years and finally exhaled.

He smiled the same way he did back in middle school, but there was something different behind it. He was a little older, a little harder, but still himself. It felt easy, like we'd paused and picked back up again.

We started talking, and I wasn't heartbroken anymore. I was home.

We fell madly in love and couldn't wait to see each other at school, after school, on the weekends. We spent every minute we could together, along with our friends, a handful of the gang was always around.

We drank what we could, smoked what we could afford, and lived like there'd never be consequences. We pooled our money to rent a hotel room where we could party. It was fun, but hard on my body — drinking too much, eating fast food, doing whatever drugs were handy. I'm surprised we survived those years.

We were as in love as two teenagers in high school could be.

I was eighteen and Mike was seventeen. He was on probation for missing too much school, and the court ordered that he be tested regularly for drugs.

After that, something shifted between us. We still loved each other, but the air felt heavier. Mike began disappearing — not physically but emotionally. Then he wouldn't answer my calls. He'd vanish for days and come back with new stories, new bruises, a thinner smile.

I told myself it was just a phase, that he'd settle down and we'd get back to what we'd been. But we never did.

I knew there was more to life. We were no longer on the same path, so I decided to break up with him. He spray-painted "I will always love you Casey" on the I-75 overpass by Carillon Park. When I drove past it, I didn't know whether to cry or smile.

For about a year after that, I didn't hear much about him. I think he went off the deep end. I heard that he was stealing stuff to sell so he could buy drugs, and that he'd had become a full-blown crackhead. He broke into a neighbor's house, and they found him asleep on their living room floor.

Then he was shot. Killed over a $20 drug deal.

His death didn't feel real at first. Just another cautionary tale whispered at parties. But this wasn't a friend-of-a-friend. This was my Mike. If I'd only been enough to keep him anchored. But I wasn't. That was just fantasy. And regret is a useless kind of hope.

He was the first boy I ever really loved. And the first one I lost.

I carry both the love and the loss—quietly, constantly—like a song only I still remember.

CHAPTER NINE

Foster

I tried to build a future with Foster before I knew what a future should feel like.

We met on the playground at Moraine Meadows in 1979, when I was in second grade, and he was in third — my brother's class. He lived in the trailer park near the Civic Center, so he wasn't technically a Dog Patcher, but we all knew each other from school. That Christmas, he played Santa Claus in our school play, and I was cast as Mrs. Claus. I thought he was one of the least attractive boys alive and was mortified. He totally had cooties. Yet, he liked me.

On the playground, he teasingly called me "Casey Doodle," and it stuck. If he saw me today, he'd call me that. Foster wasn't his real name. His aunt gave him that nickname in the hospital when he was born, and it followed him for life.

After elementary school, we barely spoke. I ignored him through most of junior high and high school, until one day, I didn't. We dated briefly, a messy, drug-fueled relationship that gutted me when it ended. When he came back around in the early 1990s, I didn't hesitate. I opened the door and didn't close it again until I had to.

I was still bleeding from losing Mike, and Foster knew it. Part of me believed it was fate — or maybe punishment. He said he wanted to try again. I didn't need much convincing.

The first few months felt like healing. He was attentive. Present. Familiar. We ate cheap food, went on long drives, talked about the past like we could rewrite it. I let myself believe it could work.

When we moved in together, we were twenty-something and playing house. We rented a Crackerbox apartment, slept on a waterbed, and ate our meals on a foosball table. I was working in the cash office at the local drug store. He trimmed trees for a living. It was simple. Messy. Ours.

Then Mike died.

And I unraveled.

Grief made me sharp. Guarded. Cold. I don't think Foster knew what to do with that version of me. I cried myself to sleep, disappeared into work and sat in silence for hours.

I didn't know what to do with him either. I started pulling away. He started drinking more. By year two, we weren't building anything. We were just surviving under the same roof.

I used to think love meant staying. That if you loved someone enough, you endured. You forgave. You sacrificed. That's what Grandma and Grandpa did, right? So, I stayed. For six long years.

We didn't fight much near the end. Not loudly. Not often. We just stopped trying. Stopped talking. Stopped expecting anything new. I'd lie awake beside him feeling more alone than I ever had in an empty bed.

One night, I cooked his favorite meal — spaghetti — just the way he liked it. He barely said thank you. Just shoveled it in, burped, and turned on the TV. I stood at the sink, hands wet, heart heavy, and I thought, this isn't it. This can't be it.

When I finally asked for a separation, he didn't argue. We agreed that I'd leave for a weekend so he could pack up his stuff. It was supposed to be clean. Simple. Done.

But that Friday, something happened at Grandma and Grandpa's house that made the universe collapse.

Police tape blocked their driveway. A mobile command unit had been set up in a parking lot down the street.

My brother was holed up in the house with a gun.

That weekend, I left more than a relationship. I left a version of myself.

And she needed to go.

Foster was the last person I tried to love without loving myself first before I understood that loving someone else doesn't count if you disappear in the process. He wasn't abusive. He wasn't evil. But he didn't show up. Not for me. Not in any of the ways that mattered. And I bent myself into silence trying to pretend that was enough.

I once believed love meant fighting through anything, that if you stayed long enough, it would all work out. But now I know that love worth keeping doesn't ask you to disappear inside it.

CHAPTER TEN

SWAT

That Friday morning, I carried a mug of coffee from the kitchen to the living room and took a last, quiet look around. Then I gathered my purse, my phone, and kept my car keys from jingling as I slipped out the door. He was still sleeping. We'd agreed to keep it peaceful. Mutual. Clean break.

In midafternoon, I got a call. Kelly's crying voice, "Casey, I need you." I was out the door.

I didn't know that Kelly had walked into the kitchen that morning, pulled a gun, and fired a shot that sent our grandparents running across the street to the neighbors, who called 911.

Kelly had had many episodes, but this one felt more dangerous, more urgent. The cracking edge of desperation in his voice told me this time would end differently. I felt it in my chest before I even got in the car.

When Kelly was struggling, he usually turned to alcohol and drugs, got shit-faced and called me crying. I always came running. I'd console him, remind him he was worthy of love and that he'd always have me.

I raced toward Gladstone Street. But when I got close, the road was blocked. So, I parked and started running. Jennifer, my closest childhood friend, stopped me on the street. Her face said everything —panic, pity, fear. We hadn't spoken in months, but at that moment, we were twelve again. "You can't go up there," she said.

"What?" My voice cracked. "Is anyone hurt? Where are Grandma and Grandpa? Is Kelly okay?"

Then I saw a tank. A fucking tank rolling down my street. It didn't look real — like a movie set that got lost in Moraine. My heart slammed in my chest. My breath caught. I couldn't move.

A man was standing up in the hatch, his weapon trained on the front door of my grandparents' house. The house with flowers in the garden and decades of love etched into its walls was a threat. Kelly was inside.

There were flashing lights, rifles drawn, and a trailer parked in Cappel's parking lot down the street.

A detective pulled me into the temporary outpost.

His questions were rapid-fire: How many guns does he have? Would he come out shooting? What state is he in?

I didn't have any answers. I only knew my brother was inside with a gun.

I knew he'd been drinking. I was pretty sure he was coked out. Capable of anything. My mouth was dry. My thoughts scattered. I heard the words but couldn't track them. I didn't know Kelly when he was like this. How the fuck should I to know what was in his arsenal? He was my brother, but I didn't keep tabs on his weapons.

Hours later, after endless tension and radio static, Kelly emerged, handcuffed and silent. They loaded him into a cruiser and drove him to the trailer. I asked if I could speak to him. When they said yes, I ran to the police car. His window was down. His eyes were wild and red.

"I love you," I said. "I'll follow the car if you want me to."

He seethed through clenched teeth, "I'll see you in hell!"

He was gone. Somebody else was using his body. I let him go. At least he was safely away from guns.

Grandma and Grandpa's house was semi-famous now — news crews everywhere. By the time I got there, the street had gone quiet, and the house glowed like a stage set. No one inside was going to sleep.

I found my grandparents in the living room, visibly shaken, with the kind of stillness that comes after the adrenaline burns off. Grandma's eyes were too tired for tears. Grandpa held an empty mug.

"Where did he shoot?" I asked.

They pointed to the hole in the kitchen floor. Small. The size of a .38 round. It's still there, even now. A tiny circle burned into the linoleum. A silent scar in the place that fed us, laughed with us, raised us.

That tiny hole could have been the death of my brother. It nearly was.

Then came the final hit. My mom had shown up drunk and out of control, screaming for her son. The cops had arrested her, too. Kelly was in custody, and I had to bail my mother out of jail.

It took all night. I returned to the apartment early Saturday morning emotionally wrecked. Physically drained. Foster was scheduled to pack up that weekend. My overnight bag was already packed for a trip to Cleveland with my neighbors. I rolled it two doors down to my friends' apartment.

The weekend I thought would mark the quiet end of one chapter had exploded into a collision of grief, trauma, and chaos.

Yet through all of it, I felt one thing more than anything else. I wasn't broken. I was done.

Done pretending. Done holding the line. Done mistaking survival for strength.

Done doesn't mean defeated.

Done means free.

Free to stop trying to make things work with people who aren't working on themselves. Free to stop carrying everyone else's chaos. Free to face the truth I'd been circling for years:

My life wasn't breaking. It had already broken.

And I could start building something real with the pieces.

With truth. With intention. With me at the center — finally.

CHAPTER ELEVEN

Travis

After the chaos of the SWAT weekend, I needed to disappear for a few days. So, we piled into my friend's little four-door grocery-getter and hit the road to Cleveland: me, Trevor, Aerin and Trevor's brother, Travis, all came along. Travis had joined us a few times before, but something about him stood out that weekend.

The first time I met him, I thought he was cute. One of our earliest connections was over the number five, which I hold sacred. We were at Trev and Aerin's place watching a college basketball game during March Madness. I don't remember the teams, but I remember Travis.

The game came down to a final three-point shot at the buzzer. The player scored, and without missing a beat, we both blurted out, "It's because he's number five."

We looked at each other, surprised, and said in unison: "Five is my favorite number."

Travis pulled a folded piece of paper from his wallet with the number five on it. "I carry this everywhere," he said. I stared. I'd loved the number five since I was a kid — something about its balance, its symmetry. Five fingers, five toes. It felt like home.

I chose that number every chance I got — at checkout lanes, gas pumps, hotel rooms. Now, here it was again, attached to a cute guy who wasn't trying to flirt with me but kept smiling all the same.

It was a small thing, but it felt like more, a tiny signpost that something different might be beginning. But the timing wasn't right. I was still married.

I was 27 and had just separated from Foster. Despite everything I'd been through, I looked and somehow felt like a vibrant young woman, finally ready to live life on her own terms.

The attention didn't stop. The boys kept coming around. I'll admit it — I like attention. I'm a Leo. I feel most alive when I'm treated like a queen. I dated. I went to clubs, had a few flings — nothing serious.

In the late 1990s and early 2000s, we didn't have Tindr — no swiping, no curated profiles. Just bar meetups, friend-of-a-friend setups, and taking chances with strangers. I wasn't looking for forever, but I also wasn't looking for empty, either, although that's mostly what I found.

Travis wasn't like the others. He was more than another fleeting distraction or momentary fix. He showed up quietly without trying too hard, without the drama and volatility I'd grown used to. He didn't ask for space in my life. He just took his place in it, like it was meant to be his. I didn't know how deep we would go, or how much we would carry together. But the second time we crossed paths, it didn't feel random. It felt like a door creaking open, asking if I was ready to walk through.

I wasn't just scared of love. I was scared of being seen. Travis didn't demand that I open up, but something about him made it impossible to hide.

After a lifetime of surviving, hiding had become my default. Grandma and Grandpa taught me to stuff everything down and never name the trauma. I'd survived trauma upon trauma without the space or tools to process it. By the time Travis came into my life, I was an expert at pretending I was fine.

What caught me off guard was that he was even better at pretending than I was. If I was the queen of putting on a happy face, Travis was, in every way, the king. His boyish grin made people believe he was all light — sports, music, jam bands, laughter. He could talk to anyone, carry a room without effort. But behind that smile lived a boy who'd been taught to bury everything.

He was raised in a house full of contradiction — a likely bipolar mother, a distant father, and silence where there should have been stability.

Travis never talked to a doctor, but I saw the signs — obsessive behavior, deep mood swings, what I now believe was undiagnosed depression and OCD. I also believe he struggled with an eating disorder. When we met, I was in full-blown anorexia-mode, so I recognized the patterns — the skipping meals, the fixation on control. It wasn't just physical, it was survival disguised as control.

I'd been wearing the caretaker role so long it fit like skin. I wasn't a partner, I was a rescuer, a witness. I didn't know that when two people haven't healed, love becomes survival in disguise. We weren't building a life, we were clinging to each other's bandages, hoping they would hold.

He proposed to me in an email. It was tax season at the CPA firm, and I was buried in deadlines when his message popped up. It was probably the most romantic thing he ever did — a poem, typed out and sent in the middle of an ordinary workday. I can't remember the exact words, but it ended with something like: "At this point in my life, I want to ask you to become my wife."

I wrote back a resounding yes.

We planned a runaway wedding three months later. On June 15, 2002 — six weeks before my thirtieth birthday — I married my second husband in Las Vegas, Nevada. It was 115 degrees that day. Walking down the strip felt like being baked in an oven. Our ceremony was simple — just the two of us and the officiant. We got married to "At the Gazebo" by Trey Anastasio. It was magical, one of my favorite days. How I wish I could go back to that day knowing what I know now.

Soon after we were married, Travis and I bought a house, a brand-new, never-been-lived-in-before house. It didn't have the basement I wanted but otherwise, it was perfect. We toured about twenty homes before we found it, and as soon as we walked through the door, we knew we wanted it. In September, we moved in and stared optimistically at our future together.

That fall passed quickly. With all the moving and decorating and unpacking into our new home, time seemed to evaporate. Suddenly, we were about to have our first Christmas at the new place.

Then the phone rang.

My mom called to tell me that Kelly was drinking heavily again. He was complaining of stomach pain, so she'd taken him to the hospital where he was admitted for testing. He was there alone. She asked if I could stop in, and I said I'd come by after work.

When I arrived at Miami Valley Hospital, the unit was quiet. A long hallway was lined with worn chairs, puzzles, and children's books stacked on the windowsill. The Critical Intensive Care Unit felt like a waiting room for grief. I got there just before Mom, Grandma, and Grandpa arrived. When I stepped into his room, I didn't see Kelly — not the way I remembered him. He was intubated, swollen, surrounded by machinery.

A ventilator hissed steadily beside him. No one was working on him. There were no beeping machines to rally hope, no nurses rushing in. Just hoses and silence.

The doctor told us there was no chance of recovery.

His pancreas had ruptured, releasing enzymes that liquefied his internal organs. He said my brother's insides were like pudding. His lungs would go next. He was being kept alive by machines, nothing more.

My knees went weak. Grandma stood beside me, stunned. Her voice trembled. "There has to be some hope he'll wake up, right?"

But there wasn't. And we knew it. We told the medical team to withhold life support and let his body go. Everyone had to sign off. Me, Grandma, Grandpa, Mom, Dad, and Missy. Amie didn't have to sign since she was under 18. There was a 72 hour wait before they could pull the plug.

That Saturday, December 14, 2002, Kelly died at the age of thirty-one, surrounded by friends and family. The grief hit me like a blackout. I lost more than my brother. I lost a part of myself. I loved him in a way that defied explanation. He'd been almost like a son to me. The ache was immediate, deep, permanent. It was like losing Mike again, but worse. I should have been able to save him, but I couldn't.

He didn't die all at once. Kelly died over years — with every drink, every pill, every time he gave up. In the end, it was suicide by surrender.

Travis was there, too. He stood awkwardly in the hallway at the hospital and looked at me helplessly as I signed the forms that would take my brother's life. He was the same at the funeral home. He hated crowds, and there were a lot of people that day. Foster was also there — he and Kelly had been best friends, and I'd asked him to be a pallbearer.

That day, it poured rain. A week before Christmas, the sky opened up in a relentless, soaking gray. The pallbearers slipped as they carried my brother's casket and nearly dropped him. I remember thinking that Foster's shoes must be ruined, but everything else is a blur.

I don't remember Christmas that year. I'm sure we celebrated with Grandma and Grandpa, but the memories are gone. Grief swallowed them whole.

However, I do recall on January 12th, 2003, we gathered for Grandma's birthday. As Travis and I were leaving, my mom said something that made me pause.

Something was off.

My period was late. I put the thought out of my mind, but a few days later, I used a pregnancy test I happened to have.

It was positive. Just like that — a heartbeat waiting in the wings of all that loss.

It didn't make sense. How could my body, soaked in grief, be carrying life? But it was. And it was everything.

I couldn't wait to tell Travis. I didn't want to bother him at work, so I taped the pregnancy test to a piece of paper and stuck it to the refrigerator with a magnet — a quiet announcement waiting to be found.

He called me as soon as he got home and saw it. He was thrilled. We both were.

We couldn't wait to get to our first doctor's appointment and hear her heartbeat. It felt like hope — like maybe, finally, something was starting fresh.

Travis stood by me during Ciera's birth. He was the only person in the room besides the medical team, present, helpful, and proud. He cut the cord, helped clean her up, and gave her her first bath. He held her, changed her, and stayed involved in every moment at the hospital.

Once we got home, everything changed. He acted like he'd never heard a baby cry before. And she cried a lot. Her colic made every night endless. Travis watched her while I showered, but handed her back to me, screaming, the second I stepped out.

This was not his first time, so I was sure he would be the one showing me the ropes. He had his daughter, London, in high school. She was born in March of 1988, so she was eleven years old when I met her. Travis seemed like a loving father who took great care of London.

That's why I was surprised at how Travis was reacting to our new baby. Ciera was born on a Saturday evening. We were discharged on Monday. By Tuesday, Travis was back at work, and I was home alone with a baby who couldn't be soothed and a thousand questions no one could answer.

Just like that, it was the Mommy and Ciera show. I was no longer a newlywed. I was a mother. And I was doing it alone.

Travis was attentive when she wasn't fussy. Four months in, we switched her to formula from breast milk, and suddenly she started sleeping. For the next six months, it was like a brand new baby. She was happy, content, sleeping and napping as she should, and we were happy. He would nap with her on his chest, watching sports from his chair.

Soon, our baby became a toddler, and she was very mischievous! I know we had a lot of fun in those days. Going to parks, going to the movies or going out for ice cream, we seemed like a real family for a while.

But depression is a relentless bastard, and it soon took hold of us both. Slowly and quietly we each sank into our old habits of isolation and numbing the pain.

We would drink and watch music videos on the weekends when we weren't with our close friends, Steve and Tamara. We loved the DVD collection that was 90% music and 10% Disney Princess. Our favorites were Pearl Jam, Seether, and Blind Melon. Of course, that didn't hold a candle to the collection of CDs we had amassed. That collection exceeded the 1000s in quantity, and the quality was amazing. We had every type of genre of music you could name was likely in our collection. We weren't big country fans, so not a lot of music there, but we had a lot of Phish, a lot of Grateful Dead, and a lot of Dave Matthews

Band. It was a thorough, well-thought-out collection that we were both super proud of.

But the music wasn't enough to hold us together. As time went on, I stayed in my cycle of silence and stuffing my emotions. I rarely talked about my lost loved ones and the traumas I faced as a child.

Travis tried in his own way. But grief like mine was a language he didn't speak. We drifted apart.

By the time Ciera was six, Travis and I had built a life of silence around each other. I worked all the time. He watched sports all the time. We didn't fight, but we fell into a rut of depression and silence.

The grief I carried was impossible to share. He was carrying his own demons. We stopped being a couple and became roommates. With each passing day, the distance between us widened, until one day he asked if I wanted to leave, to end the marriage. I said I'd been thinking about it. He had, too. We decided we'd try to find happiness apart.

It was silly. We should have gone to counseling. I don't know why we didn't try. We loved each other the best way we knew how, but it just wasn't enough.

We separated in November of 2009. I moved back to Grandma's house with Ciera, and we took turns with our daughter, keeping her every other week. We got along well and were very kind to one another. I dated. He dated. We each ended up with someone we regretted. Shortly before my birthday in 2010, I began flirting with Travis again, hoping we could start talking about a relationship. I missed him. I missed us. I missed a family for my daughter. But it wasn't meant to be.

He was in a difficult relationship with someone half his age who was also a close friend of London's, which created a huge rift between them. The girlfriend swooped in and took my place as swiftly as she could at the house. None of his friends or family understood his situation. I know he must have been eaten up on the inside and was feeling trapped. I found out later he had tried to break up with her, but she threatened to harm herself, so he stayed.

I didn't know about her while I was text flirting with him. I would have backed off if I had known he was with someone. I was still waiting for a text back from him one night when I fell asleep holding my phone. Before five in the morning on August 4, 2010, my cell phone startled me awake. I didn't want to wake Grandma and Ciera, so I stepped onto the back porch to take the call. It was a detective with the Montgomery County Sheriff's office. They'd responded to a call about a shot fired at my home in Union.

When the police arrived, they found Travis still holding the gun, killed by a single, self-inflicted wound.

He'd been in the driver's seat of his Jeep, parked in our garage. The girlfriend, who was sleeping over, heard the shot, found Travis, and ran to a neighbor's house to call the police.

I told the detective this must be a sick, twisted joke, but his voice stayed steady. "Ma'am, I'm so sorry. It's real."

He asked if I wanted to talk to Trevor who was there on scene. I asked if my sister-in-law, Aerin, was also there and he put her on the phone.

Aerin took the phone, confirming everything the detective had told me. I began having a panic attack and paced back and forth along the sidewalk behind the house.

It didn't make sense. I'd talked to Travis the day before, and we'd made plans for Ciera the following week. He'd be on vacation, and he had tickets for Phish. With amazing things in the very near future, why kill himself? Why not after vacation? After the show? It didn't compute.

Later, we learned he'd been taking antidepressants — not prescribed but given to him by his girlfriend. Some of those meds list suicidal ideation as a side effect, especially in people who are not medically monitored.

We believe he woke up with suicidal thoughts he couldn't control and went through with it. I knew he'd been depressed but never imagined he'd take it this far. He'd seen fallout in our family after my mom did the same thing.

I like to think he didn't mean it. That he woke up lost inside a chemically induced fog and couldn't find his way out.

But whether it was a choice or a symptom, the outcome is the same. Ciera and London lost their dad. And I lost the only man who ever made me believe in magic.

CHAPTER TWELVE

London

I met Travis's daughter, London, on a sunny afternoon at Aerin and Trevor's apartment. We were celebrating something —a birthday — or maybe it was just one of our classic get-togethers. I brought my often-requested Mexican layer dip, and Aerin baked a cake. Travis was there, and so was London.

She was eleven at the time, all skinny limbs and wide-eyed charm. I loved her instantly. She was bright, funny, full of life. Not shy at all. Within minutes, we struck up a conversation about shoes. I told her I liked hers, and she said she liked mine, too. It was easy — natural.

When Travis and I started dating, I thought a lot about my own stepmother, Teresa, who treated me like family even before marrying my dad. I followed her example and treated London like she was mine from the beginning.

I would've spent every weekend with her, if I could, but Travis had limited visitation rights, and he wasn't one to fight it in court. Besides, London was growing up fast — a total social butterfly, always off to a sleepover or sporting event. Then, I blinked, and she wasn't a kid anymore.

She'd spent most of her childhood living with her mom, Missy, and stepdad, Rick, so we didn't see her as often as we would have liked. But when Ciera was born, a new world opened. London adored her baby sister. She brought her little gifts and trinkets, took her for haircuts and on shopping trips, and showed up in all the ways that mattered.

Being a mother figure to London changed me. It gave me practice and perspective. I was still so young, yet I got to love her in a way that helped me grow into the kind of mom I wanted to be. She taught me as much as I taught her.

When she had boy troubles, she confided in me. We had long talks at the house in Union, sprawled on the couch, figuring life out. Watching her grow up taught me how quickly childhood passes and how important it is to give kids a soft landing place, something I didn't always have growing up.

Teresa was that soft place for me, although our visits were infrequent, and I made sure London knew that she had that in me. Even when we disagreed. Even after her dad and I split and she drifted away. I never stopped loving her.

We found our way back, and that was beautiful. We came back to each other when it mattered most. Now, we're the best of friends.

I watch her mothering her own stepdaughter, Gabby, and I'm filled with pride. She's doing it with grace, humor, and heart, breaking her own cycles. I couldn't be prouder.

Ciera

When I found out I was pregnant, we were still raw from losing Kelly. It didn't make sense. How could my body carry life in the midst of so much death? But there she was, growing inside me.

My pregnancy was textbook. I had hardly any illness, just fatigue. No morning sickness. Most of the time I felt good, and I loved being pregnant. I still miss the feeling of a baby kicking.

Travis was great during that phase. He came to every appointment and ultrasound. He didn't say much, but I could tell he cared. I knew he wanted a boy, and when the doctor said, "It's a girl," I saw it hit him. He never said anything, but it left him a little disappointed.

Travis lived and breathed sports. ESPN was always on in our house. He sometimes bet on games

— football, basketball, baseball. No matter what sport it was, if it involved a score, he'd watch it. He wanted a son to carry on that tradition.

Until his senior year when an injury benched him, he'd been starting quarterback at Wayne High School. That year, he got a cheerleader pregnant, and when the baby was born, they moved in with his mom. It didn't last. When London was just a few months old, the cheerleader and their baby moved out.

This was his second baby, his second girl. No son to carry his name. Just London and Ciera. And Travis didn't know how to connect with either of them. He disappeared into his games, his bets, his stats. He even watched golf.

He displayed most of his sports memorabilia in our home office — shelves of autographed balls, jerseys, plaques, and framed magazine covers. I didn't much mind. He took pride in that room, and he kept it clean. He kept everything clean.

Travis never got a diagnosis, but I'm certain he had OCD. Our house was always spotless. I loved it until I hated it, because I couldn't make a mess without triggering his reaction.

Scrapbooking was a problem. Laundry piles were a problem. Raising a kid in that kind of environment? An entirely different challenge.

We never had playdough or messy finger painting. Daycare handled that. His perfection left little room for a baby.

Ciera was born on a Saturday — September 6, 2003 — eight days before her due date. She was full-term, healthy, and beautiful. A happy little baby. Until we got her home.

When the colic started, I called it the witching hour. Travis worked early shifts — 2:30 a.m. most days — so he'd head to bed around 7 or 8 p.m. I'd get him settled, and almost like clockwork, she'd start crying. And crying. And crying.

I thought she didn't like me. No joke. Every cry felt like rejection. I'd bounce her, sing to her, cry quietly beside her crib — nothing worked. It wasn't just exhaustion. It was heartbreak.

Mom and I weren't on very good terms during my pregnancy, so I didn't have a mother to call or stay with me. I didn't have a village. I just had Travis, and he went back to work right after she was born, leaving me alone with the scream machine.

She wasn't satisfied with breast milk. At four months we switched her to formula and, almost immediately, she slept through the night. Life became easier, and we settled into a routine.

But something had already shifted.

Maybe I missed the signs with Travis. He showed up when it was exciting — the ultrasounds, the gear, the idea of a baby. But once the crying started and I needed him most, he disappeared into sports.

Sometimes, I wondered if he was jealous — not of Ciera— but of how completely she owned me. My time, my energy, my sleep. There was nothing left over for him. I think he resented that, and I can't blame him.

He loved her — I know he did — but he didn't know how to love her in the way she needed to be loved, and he couldn't show up for me. His love was quiet. Distant. Conditional, maybe. Maybe he was just unfamiliar with the chaos of newborn life.

He helped around the house. The lawn always looked perfect. The trash was always out. Dishes rarely sat in the sink. But the baby was my department.

I was too busy surviving it to resent him.

She was mine — all mine. Travis had the yard, the house, and his sports. I had Ciera, a full-time job, and I was working my way through college. I didn't have much left to give him.

Our marriage quietly slipped off the radar. I didn't neglect it out of resentment. I was pulled in too many directions and thought I was doing the best I could.

I tried to be the best possible mom. I read the books, did the research, and I trusted my instincts. Most people I talked to were into 'Ferberizing' — teaching babies to self-soothe in their own cribs. Not me. I felt safest with her sleeping beside me, and she felt safest with me. That's what mattered.

When Ciera was three years old, I began taking her to dance classes. She was a beautiful little ballerina, but she didn't like the attention of the end of year recital. We convinced her she could do it, and she begrudgingly did.

She took classes for four years, but when Travis passed, they didn't seem so important. When she told me she didn't want to do it anymore, I didn't pressure her. I knew she wasn't likely to become a prima ballerina.

Our separation was hard for her. She was six and didn't understand. I didn't expect her to and simply explained that we'd be living at Grandma's house and that Dad and I would trade off each week so we got equal time with her.

She enjoyed spending time with her dad but always called me to say goodnight. It had to be confusing for her. I hate that I put her through that.

When Travis died, the first thing I thought of was how I'd tell my daughter she'd never see her dad again.

It was a chance to break the cycle of silence I'd inherited, but I didn't have the words, so I decided to ask for help.

I reached out to HR at work. I explained that Travis had passed, so I'd need to take a few days off. Then I asked her what to say to my daughter. She didn't have the answer, but she knew who would. One of our employee benefits was the opportunity to consult a licensed psychiatrist, and she got me an appointment the same day.

As soon as I hung up with HR, London called. We hadn't spoken since the separation, but she needed to hear it from my lips.

Her crying voice on the other end asked, "Is it true?" And I had to tell her, yes, her dad was truly gone. We decided to meet at the house in Union later that morning.

I had to straighten myself up for the rest of that God-forsaken day, so I decided to do what I did best, what I'd been trained to do since I was a toddler. I pretended nothing had happened. I woke Ciera as though it was any other morning, got her dressed, and dropped her off at day camp at the Civic Center. I put my emotions on pause and tried to act as though nothing had changed.

I decided I'd better let Grandma know, so I called her from the car — probably not the best way to give her the news, but I'd arranged to meet with HR at the house in Union at nine that morning to discuss next steps, so the phone call had to suffice.

Grandma loved Travis dearly and was upset when we split up. The news of his death devastated her. I asked her to be delicate with Ciera, and not to mention that her father had taken his own life.

Then I called my dad, whom I hadn't spoken with in a while. He loved Travis, and I knew he would want to know. I said that since I didn't have a mom I could call, I'd decided to call him.

He was kind and caring and gave me words of comfort as I sobbed into the phone. I appreciated the companionship during the twenty-five-minute drive to Union. It was good to hear his voice.

Some members of my team at work arrived at the house in Union to help me sort out what to do next. Our conversation was awkward, to say the least, but they got to work on their phones and arranged a service to remove the Jeep so I wouldn't have to see the place where Travis took his life.

I am forever grateful to my past employer and my friends at work, who stayed until the tow truck came. They let me talk openly without passing judgement and were a great comfort to me.

When my co-workers left, London and Travis's mom, Dee, arrived. We hugged, cried, and started going through the house together. I hadn't been inside for about six months, but nothing had changed. Every picture, every decoration was still in its spot, clean and presentable. I thought Travis must have cleaned that day.

I needed time, but I had an appointment with the psychiatrist. I hugged Dee and London and cried again. They asked if they could stay behind and grieve a little longer and I told them to lock up on their way out.

At two that afternoon, I was in a tiny room explaining to a complete stranger that my estranged husband had taken his own life in the garage of our family home, and that I'd have to explain that to a six year old in a way that wouldn't permanently damage her psyche.

The psychiatrist's response was simple. If you don't want to traumatize her, don't make it traumatic. Be honest without over telling the truth. No matter what you say, she'll always remember it, so whatever you do, don't lie to her.

That smacked me right across the face. Honesty? How do I pull that off? I practiced with the doctor. He said it would all be okay and that he was available on a regular basis if I was interested.

In the hallway at the Civic Center on my way to pick up Ciera, I ran into one of the day camp instructors and pulled her aside. I told her the news, said I was going to tell Ciera, and wasn't sure she'd be at camp the next day. She hugged me briefly and said they'd call me if Ciera got upset while she was there.

When she saw me, Ciera grabbed her backpack and skipped to the door. "Hi Mommy!" Big hugs from such a little girl. I was nervous and decided to get her buckled into the car before I told her.

I let her ride up front. My face must have shown what was about to come out of my mouth, because she asked, "What's wrong?"

I said, "I've got really sad news, and I am not sure how to tell you. Honey, your daddy's body quit working last night. He's died and gone to Heaven."

She was silent for a moment, then looked at me like I had two heads.

"What do you mean?"

I took her hands in mine and said it again in a very matter-of-fact tone, sounding as calm as I could to avoid traumatizing her. "His body stopped working, sweetheart. He's gone to Heaven now. We won't be able to talk to him or see him anymore."

She began to sob. "Daddy?"

"Yes, baby, your daddy is gone. It's just me and you now."

"So, he's gone to Heaven?"

Heaven was a concept she'd learned a few months before when we'd lost our cat, Jerry, her first exposure to death. She was too young to remember Mom and Grandpa's passings, but at least she'd had the cat experience, so she knew what it meant to never see them again. She cried for a few minutes, while I hugged her tightly and told her that I loved her and so did Daddy.

Her innocent little face overcome with sadness is frozen in my memory. Then a thought occurred to her. "Mommy, do you think Jesus needed something cleaned and that's why Daddy had to go to Heaven?"

I couldn't help it. I burst into laughter, and she laughed with me. Just like that, we went from tears to laughter.

"Does this mean I can have McDonalds for dinner?"

I said of course and drove straight to McDonalds. She could have anything she wanted. What a mature way to rationalize her dad's passing. I was consumed by grief, but I smiled at the precious little heart sitting beside me.

A few days later, arrangements were made with the funeral home. We had his body cremated, so there was a gathering, but no viewing. Ciera came and said something that took me aback. "Mommy, give me your phone. I'm going to call Daddy just to see if he answers."

"Oh honey, Daddy can't answer his phone. He isn't here anymore. His body quit working, and he went to Heaven."

I pondered her request, then I went to my room and pulled out the bag the funeral home had given me with his clothes, his watch, his wallet and keys, and the hemp necklace I'd made for him many years ago. He never took it off. I still have it, although the hemp is now discolored and blood-stained.

I found his phone and took it into Ciera's room, which was once my room. I decided to tell her that she would be seven on her next birthday and that when I was little, I lay in that bed and saw the number 7 outlined by shadows and doorways.

She asked again. "Can I call Daddy?" I showed her his phone. I said I had his wallet and keys and the necklace, and the clothes he was wearing. She was devastated, because she realized that if I had those things, her daddy must really be gone. She burst into tears and hugged me tightly, which tore me apart. I started crying, too, and we sat there holding each other and crying.

I think it finally sunk in that the situation was permanent. Her time with her father was just memories, now. No more going back to the "old house," as she called it.

At the funeral, there was no casket, no ashes, just pictures of Travis and notes and flowers and gifts. Ciera came early to see everything before the guests arrived. I sent her home with Teresa so I could greet the swarm who came to show their respect for Travis.

It was a huge turnout, as Travis would have pointed out to me, I'm sure. Ciera was sad to leave. She still gives me shit about not letting her attend the funeral, but I was afraid someone would say something about suicide.

After the funeral, Ciera and I moved back into the house in Union. I felt closer to Travis there, and I think the continuity was important for Ciera.

The next year, she was a first grader at St. Christopher's in Vandalia. We spent the year packing up and preparing to sell the house. I felt sad every time I pulled into the garage; I couldn't get the image of him lying dead in his Jeep out of my head. The following spring, I started looking for a house to rent for the next few years until I regained my footing.

We found a place in Miami Township on Southlea Drive behind Smash Burger and Smoothie King, within walking distance of a Target near the Dayton Mall, and a ten-minute drive to Grandma. The big, fenced back yard would be perfect for an above ground pool.

Ciera started second grade in Miamisburg. She'd

have to make new friends and take the bus to school, which must have been both exciting and scary for her, but she took it like a champion. We soon discovered that a girl in her class lived in the house next door. What a blessing!

That first summer, things were good. I started dating Grant, and he soon moved into the house. He tried to engage with Ciera, but they didn't seem to speak the same language. At first, she thought he was funny, but that didn't last long, and she began spending more time with friends.

Then I became pregnant, and Max came along. Grant and I took Ciera to the ultrasound exam when we discovered the baby's gender. She'd wanted a baby sister badly, and she wasn't happy he'd be a boy. She'd recently lost her dad, and now she'd have a new step-dad and baby brother she'd hadn't asked for. But she fell in love with Max the moment he was born. I have the sweetest pictures of nine-year-old Ciera holding him in the NICU.

As she grew up, she sometimes asked about her dad's death. Did he have cancer? Did he have the flu? Why did his body quit working? I tried to reply honestly. "Mommy's not ready to talk to you about that yet. Can you ask me again later?" And for a time, that satisfied her.

But when she was eleven, she said, "Mom, I'm old enough now. I want to know what happened to my dad." I looked into the eyes of my little girl and realized she wasn't so little anymore. It was time to tell her the truth. All of it.

I let her know that her dad suffered from depression, which is an illness, but he wouldn't go to a doctor to help it. I said that my brother had sold her father a gun, and that I thought he was sleepwalking when he went to his closet and took the gun from a shelf, then went to his car, sat down and shot himself.

It was out. The words hung in the air like fog.

"What?" She was unable to digest what I'd just fed her and began sobbing.

I explained that I didn't think he meant to do it. He had a vacation coming up and had made plans to spend time with her. He had concert tickets for Phish. He wouldn't have left all those things behind on purpose. It must have been an accident. To this day, I believe that's true, that he should still be here.

She cried and cried, then we hugged and she straightened herself up, just like she had seen me do so many times. I encouraged her to let it out, to not keep it inside, to not stuff the emotions down that surely were welling up inside her. I wasn't scared of the truth anymore. I was scared of her repeating my past of not expressing herself.

The years from eleven to sixteen were difficult for her and she went through some rough stages. She'd been an only child and had to adjust to sharing her mother with a brother who had special needs and sharing her home with a man with whom she had no relationship at all.

In her eyes, Grant was an intruder. I encouraged them to spend time together, but they never clicked. At best, they tolerated each other, and I was stuck in the middle.

I guess they shouldn't have expected much from me. I was consumed with work and Max, unable to carve out time for my husband and daughter. For about ten years, I rarely slept more than four or five hours a night and was constantly tired. I was late finishing my work so often, I'm surprised I wasn't fired.

Somehow, Ciera and I remained close. We enjoyed ourselves alone whenever possible, and I helped with her homework. She was a good student, a good kid, but she didn't like our living arrangements.

In 2016, we moved to a bigger house — still in Miamisburg, so Ciera could stay in the same school district. One of her long-time friends, Cadie, lived with us for a few years, so Ciera got to have a sister in some ways.

Cadie was a good kid until things went haywire, and I had to ask her to move back in with her mom. At sixteen, Ciera got a boyfriend, Kam, and they stayed together for four years — until they were twenty. When they broke up, I don't think either of them was prepared for how badly it would hurt, but I was glad because I knew she was not living to her full potential while she was with him.

Kam kept her to himself and was more controlling than I realized. Ciera wanted the freedom to see friends and family. She needed a breath of fresh air.

Grant and I were not getting along, and in the summer of 2019, he moved out. Ciera had never been close to him, so I think she was relieved.

Now at twenty-one, she's a stunning mix of her dad's best features and mine, a true original. Although we hit some rough patches during her teen years, we love each other fiercely, and most days, we're best friends. Our relationship is stronger, closer — unbreakable. I wouldn't change anything about it.

She still lives at home and helps me with her brother. She's my only backup for him. She frequently goes out with friends, but she knows I worry and calls to let me know where she is and who she's with.

Her childhood scrapbook is still tucked in my closet, reminding me that the little girl who once needed me for everything now chooses me every day.

That's all the healing I need.

CHAPTER FOURTEEN

Grant

I don't remember the night we met. After Travis's funeral I'd gone to Ziggy's, the neighborhood bar, and gotten shitfaced. I was numb — floating through people and prayers I couldn't really hear. My sister, Missy, who was working a shift there that night, insisted I come.

When Grant was introduced to me, I was face-down bawling on the counter. He said he would have approached me, but he was letting me "marinate." I was still a solid mess.

Drinking had become a way of coping, and I could do it safely at Ziggy's, because my sister worked there and we'd become close friends.

About six months after Travis died, Grant and I started doing karaoke together at Ziggy's. He was full of life and laughter and told the best stories. He was overweight — not my type at all — but I looked past that.

When we'd been seeing each other for a few weeks, we'd had too much to drink and he asked if he could stay the night, Ciera and I were still living at Grandma's and I told him yes, but he'd have to be careful not to wake them up.

The next morning, we woke up laughing. I called in sick to work. The mood was light, and Ciera was excited to go out for pancakes with us. But before we could get to the restaurant, Grant went to check his phone that was left in the car overnight and came back pale. "Something's wrong," he said. "I have fifteen missed calls from my mom."

The night before, we'd been singing karaoke with his brother, Brian, at Ziggy's. Brian left the bar at the same time we did, but he never made it home. He'd switched to water early in the evening, so he wasn't drunk, but something caused him to lose control of the car. He connected with a tree and died instantly. Grant and I were the last people who saw him.

I began to wonder if an angel of death was following me.

I offered to drive Grant home so he could be on the phone in the car, and that thrust me into his family.

His mom, his sister, Tara, her twin toddlers, and his older brother, Mark, were at the house when we got there, all of them crying, shocked, in the first stage of grief. No one believed it.

They all wanted to retrace his steps. Grant assured them he hadn't been drunk. He must have swerved to miss a deer or something.

And just like that, I was part of the family. That was in May of 2011. From then on, Grant and I were together. In August, he moved into the house on Southlea, and in November, we found out we were pregnant.

I zipped back into mommy-mode, quit smoking and drinking and began eating healthier. It was a tough pregnancy. I felt sick, always exhausted, and threw up every day. What was this baby doing to me?

When I delivered Ciera, I was thirty-one. At thirty-nine, pregnancy was different. Because of I was "AMA" an advance maternal age, a neonatal specialist was assigned to monitor my pregnancy.

I thought I was struggling because of my age, but at twenty weeks, we were told this wasn't a normal pregnancy. Max had abnormalities in his brain and heart. He started kicking me like a karate champion trying to break free of the womb.

Grant supported me during the pregnancy but

didn't slow down his partying. He was out several nights a week. Instead of sharing the experience with a devoted partner, I was feeling alone.

When I was in my sixth month of pregnancy, and we knew Max would be born with abnormalities, we decided to get married. We weren't sure what to expect. From the amniocentesis, the doctors knew the baby had a chromosome disorder but that was about all they could tell us.

Grant was a grown man physically, but emotionally, he was still a child — impulsive, irresponsible, incapable of real partnership. We had a special needs son, my fatherless daughter, bills to pay and a home to run, but he never grew up.

He worked as a DJ for a while, but the business didn't go anywhere. Then he was an Uber driver and became a full-blown LLC with a staff and a fleet of three vehicles — with my financial backing and business acumen at his disposal.

We built that business with his sweat and energy, and it did well enough to pay for itself, but never made a profit of more than a few thousand dollars a year. My earnings covered the household bills and financed his enterprise.

One night when I was seven months pregnant, Grant didn't come home. I found him at Diamonds, a nude strip bar near the house and took my big belly there. He was getting a lap dance. I don't know why I didn't bail on him then, but I didn't.

After Max was born, he became even more distant. By the time Max was three, we were fighting a lot, and I suggested we separate. Grant flipped out. He insisted things could improve. I told him I needed his help around the house and with Max.

I was working fifty to sixty hours a week, taking care of Ciera and getting Max to his abundance of medical appointments. By the time he was four, he'd seen more than thirty specialists, and I'd taken him to all those appointments alone, because Grant had been busy with work or needed to sleep so he could work the night shift. He was never there when I needed him, and his drinking continued to get worse.

In 2018 when Max was six, he had major surgery to reconstruct his hips. It was a horrific experience. During the week we were in the hospital, Grant showed up once.

I was alone for all the surgeries, all the seizures, all the near-death experiences, and I resented Grant so much for making me carry the load. I began to despise his drinking and watching my hard-earned money go up in smoke.

After the surgery, Max spent weeks in full leg casts. I

decided to step down as Accounting and Tax Manager for the company I'd been with for seventeen years. I was unable to keep up with the workload, and Max needed me to be home with him. It was a difficult decision, but the right thing to do.

I couldn't continue to leave Max in daycare, so I started looking for work-from-home positions. In the spring of 2019, I found a software consulting job. It seemed like a perfect fit.

Grant kept drinking. working on his business and losing money. He said he'd lose his mind if I couldn't keep the house cleaner. I reminded him that he lived there too, and half the mess was his.

In his defense, at some point, I'd given up on housework. Every room was cluttered and dirty. The house looked like a tornado had whipped through it. But I refused to do the housework on my own.

We started fighting about how Ciera was being raised. I was lax with the rules and regulations, a "pick your battles" mom who didn't freak out over the small stuff. But Grant was concerned with what other people thought of my parenting style. He insisted I let her do too much and that I needed to put my foot down and whip her into shape. Sorry, but that's just not my style.

Because of those differences, Grant issued an

ultimatum: either I'd listen to him, or he'd divorce me. I told him to go ahead.

In July of 2019, he moved out, and I was relieved not to have to deal with his negative energy and alcohol abuse. I felt I'd been trapped in a loveless marriage.

I once believed love was something you fought to keep. Now I know that real love doesn't require you to lose yourself. Grant wasn't my future. He was just another lesson in how deeply I needed to heal, a detour through codependence disguised as comfort. Some people come into your life to show you what you no longer must accept.

CHAPTER FIFTEEN

Max

My Max. Brave and strong. Happy and content. The epitome of joy wrapped in a little boy's body. For all his issues, he brings light to this world.

But the world isn't equipped to handle kids like Max, so I've had to advocate for him and navigate the waters of special needs parenting, half the time without knowing what I'm doing. Max is non-verbal. He requires a wheelchair and lives with significant developmental delays. He is thirteen-years-old, but in many ways, he's still an infant.

When I was pregnant with him, an ultrasound showed that one side of his brain was significantly larger than the other. There were concerns about his heart and he had fluid in his head where brain matter should be.

We were referred to Cincinnati Children's Hospital for a full day of testing: fetal MRI, fetal echocardiogram, bloodwork. I lay on my side for hours during the MRI, feeling like a pincushion and test subject. Then they sent us home to wait.

A few days later, we returned and were ushered into a conference room where a team of doctors — neurology, cardiology, genetics — sat around a table like a tribunal. The neurosurgeon spoke first. Then the others. I don't remember much of what they said. Their words blurred under the weight of my shock. After that appointment, I decided to marry Grant who was the closest thing to a partner I had. I was scared and overwhelmed, and I needed someone beside me.

As the pregnancy progressed, new issues emerged. I was carrying too much amniotic fluid — a sign that Max wasn't swallowing in the womb like he should be. They said he might have feeding issues after birth. I began seeing my OB weekly.

My sisters threw me a baby shower in June. I was huge, uncomfortable, and counting the days. The next morning, at my routine OB checkup. I measured forty-two weeks — but I was only at week thirty-four. All that fluid. All that pressure. They hooked me up to monitors. I was in labor and didn't realize it.

What I thought were cramps were actually

contractions. I was sent straight to Southview Hospital. It was June 18th, and he wasn't due until the end of July.

I'd been scheduled to train my work replacement that day. Instead, I was giving birth. Ten hours later, I was told that I wasn't progressing. I'd stalled at six centimeters. The baby was having issues. They prepped me for a C-section.

Max was born in room five, five weeks and five days early. He weighed five pounds. Fives everywhere. I knew he was special.

I barely saw his face before they took him to the NICU. He wasn't crying. He wasn't breathing well. I was told to rest, but I couldn't.

The next few days were a blur of wires, alarms, monitors, and whispered conversations. Grant was in and out. Mostly, I was alone. I sat by Max's crib, watching his chest rise and fall, counting each breath, terrified it would stop. He had to be tube-fed. He struggled to swallow.

Tests upon tests confirmed what they had suspected: Max had a rare chromosomal disorder. An unbalanced translocation. One deletion. One duplication. One in the world.

We didn't get a full diagnosis until after his birth. Cord blood confirmed it: deletion 2q37.3, duplication

7q32-36.1. The geneticist said she couldn't find anyone else with his exact combination. Max was one of one. He wasn't just rare. He was singular.

We named him Maximilian Alexander. Strong name. Warrior name.

From the moment he came home, our lives revolved around Max's care: feedings, therapies, appointments. He aspirated fluid and got sick constantly. RSV, flu, pneumonia, two surgeries — all before age two. We were frequent flyers to Dayton Children's Hospital. I learned how to work suction machines, administer nebulizers, and keep emergency contacts posted to the fridge.

But there was joy, too. Max's smile. The way he responded to music. His laugh — deep and infectious. He was late for every milestone, but when they came, they were miracles. Holding his head up. Rolling over. Reaching for toys. Every inch of progress was hard-earned and hard-won.

Grant didn't handle the pressure well. He started going out more, drinking more, leaving me to care for a medically fragile baby and a grieving daughter on my own.

People talk about motherhood like it's a choice. But for me, it was more than that — it was a reckoning. A refinement. I was being melted down and reforged. Max wasn't just my son. He was the mirror I couldn't look away from, showing me every crack, every strength I'd never known I had.

And he saved me.

As long as I'm alive, he'll never have to face it alone. That's my promise to him, and to the version of me that needed that same protection long ago. His life may be rare, but it's rich. And I get to be his mother.

That's the miracle.

CHAPTER SIXTEEN

Casey

It took me a long time to realize that I hadn't been living my life. I'd been surviving everyone else's.

Grandma's grief. Kelly's rage. Mom and Dad's abandonment. Travis's depression. Grant's immaturity. And Max's complex needs. All of it lived in my body. I carried it like a second spine, invisible to the world but impossible to set down.

I was the one who paid the bills, picked up the pieces, made sure the house didn't fall. I was the structure holding up everyone else's collapse.

My life was filled with negative self-talk and self-destructive behavior. Beginning in my early teens, I experimented with pot, alcohol, mushrooms and LSD. I loved the sensation of euphoria that came with the psychedelics, but pot and alcohol were cheaper and easier to acquire. So those were my drugs of choice throughout my teens.

In my late teens, I went to a Grateful Dead show at Buckeye Lake near Columbus with my brother and some friends. We arrived early that morning, pulling into the parking lot around nine and were greeted by a swarm of hippies. Shakedown Street, as we called the vendors' tent area, was hopping and those who had camped there overnight were just waking up. Dead shows were perfect for stocking up on acid and mushrooms, and we'd brought our entire weekly paychecks with us.

We were all excited. We'd borrowed a van so we could take a truckload of friends—my dear friend, Jennifer, my brother, Kelly, my boyfriend at the time, Mike and others I don't remember.

Jennifer and I got hair wraps and walked around Shakedown buying jewelry and whatnot. Someone in our group ended up scoring acid and we found someone selling Vodka-soaked watermelon for a $1. All I ate that day was LSD and watermelon vodka. No wonder I had a bad trip. The sun was beating on us without shade and I'm prone to sun-poisoning.

Jennifer and I went into the show and wandered through the sea of hippies toward the music. We may have had the only two tickets.

I kept saying I just wanted to "follow the light," and Jennifer had to turn me around to go back to the van. The light was the sun. I wanted to walk toward it. I sat in the grass near our crew facing the sunset, feeling like I was being left behind.

I wanted to follow the Dead to their next show. I didn't have money for tickets, but I didn't care. If Jennifer hadn't been there, I might have followed them around all summer. I remember Kelly asking, "What if she doesn't snap out of it? What am I going to tell Grandma and Grandpa?"

They gave me water, which did my body a lot of good, and as I came down from the acid high I found myself in the back of the van driving home, braiding Jennifer's hair and chain-smoking. Afterward, I shook off the dust from the road and slept for two solid days. That's when I decided to stop doing acid.

I don't regret my teen years, because they helped shape me into the woman I've become, but I wish I'd taken it easy on the psychedelics. I know I killed a plethora of brain cells.

In my twenties, Foster and I drank and smoked. We went to bars on the weekends and became members of the Moose Lodge in Miamisburg. We hung out with Mom at her farm and Kelly often came over to play guitar and have a few drinks. When I began taking classes at Sinclair with my mom, I was working, sometimes two jobs, and going to school, so I slowed down my partying.

We didn't have much, but we had each other. Our little apartment on Linden Ave was tiny, but it was enough. After a while, I noticed that Foster was still doing a lot of partying while I was working so hard, and I began to resent him for not trying harder.

We were just kids when we moved in together. I think I might have been drawn to him because we had grief and trauma in common, so he felt comfortable. Easy. He'd lost his mother as a young teenager and was raised by his grandparents in the trailer courts. We'd gone to the same schools, ridden the same buses, and hung out in the summers at the Civic Center where he became a prize-winning pool player.

We both knew a boy from school named David Rowell who lived on Kreitzer Rd., adjacent to the Civic Center and trailer courts. David's younger sister, Christa, was in my elementary school class. She was homely, too thin, and seemed sad and lonely most of the time. We were friends, but I don't remember much about her. David was also a little backward, and I think he got on other people's nerves. But he didn't deserve what happened to him.

In early February 1982, Kelly and I were spending

the weekend with our dad and Teresa, so we didn't go to the Friday night movie playing at the Civic Center as we usually did. But Foster was there, and after, he recognized David by his small stature and the winter coat he was wearing. It was frigid night, but we kids walked to the center in the winter, anyway.

Foster was the last person to see David alive. When he went missing the center became a whirlwind of activity, and everyone was on edge. Then came the shocking news that the police and David's father had found a bag containing his body while searching the field near the highway behind the center.

That Sunday, someone called Dad to tell him, and he turned to Kelly and me to ask if we knew the boy. He must not have known what to say about his body being found in a bag, so he told us that David froze to death. Later that day, he took us home to Grandma and Grandpa's house. They already knew what happened but didn't say anything. We saw it on the TV news. His body had been mutilated and was found in pieces. Moraine police investigated and eventually a boy from the trailer park went to prison for the murder.

After that, I was afraid to go to the Civic Center and never went alone.

David's tragic death unsettled the community. People started locking their doors and children were no longer allowed to play outside alone. It struck a chord with everyone we knew. We all slept a little less soundly.

Many years later, there was a private investigation. The lead investigator, Jack Barnhart, wrote a book, ... *And Then There Was Reasonable Doubt: The State of Ohio v. Charles 'Keith' Wampler,* in which he maintains that others, including David's father, may have been involved, that Keith Wampler was wrongly convicted.

The story still gives me the sick feeling that something is horribly wrong with this world. But at the age of nine, it was overwhelming. It robbed me of my innocence, my feeling of safety, and sense of belonging.

I grew up near a murder scene. I played in the fields where David's corpse was found. I walked through that trailer court. I can't imagine what it must have been like for my grandparents, who must have worried every time we left the house.

From that point on that trauma was a part of life. I was taught to be quiet and keep going through the motions. In those days, we didn't have grief counselors, so we had to figure it out on our own and hide our feelings.

The private detective interviewed Foster whose testimony supported the idea that Keith hadn't killed

David, because of the time when he saw David. That murder put Dog Patchers and trailer park kids into the same skin, bonded by our fear. Our grief. Our trauma.

So, Foster and I shared many of the same traumas and numbed our pain with drugs, alcohol and silence. We grew apart because we couldn't find the words to keep us together.

My marriages with Travis, and with Grant ran the same course — a honeymoon phase followed by too much partying, then resentment because we were unable to share our feelings.

By the time Grant moved out in 2019, I was a mess. Too many years of trudging through my life without getting enough sleep or taking care of my body caught up with me. And the strain of being a single parent to Ciera and Max took a toll.

My unraveling didn't come with sirens or explosions but with quiet resignation. I quit the job I'd loved and excelled at for seventeen years and decided to work from home so I could get Max on and off the bus. I'd kept up the pace of a full-time job and full-time parenting as long as I could.

Then in January of 2020, my life fell apart. I was struggling with my job and started having physical symptoms. My gall bladder had been removed in 2006, but I began having severe pain in my right side where it had been, and I was nauseous all the time. At first I thought I had a stomach flu, but the pain got worse, and the nausea never ended.

I continued to work full-time but I was falling farther and farther behind. By the end of January, I could barely function. I was taking care of Max, work was killing me, and the housework was piling up. I was in pain, severely depressed, and needed help.

My doctor ran multiple tests, but couldn't find anything, so he ordered a CT scan, which revealed a small mass on my right kidney. An MRI raised the suspicion of cancer. A full nephrectomy — removal of my kidney and adrenal gland on the right side — was recommended. I'd be left with one good kidney and another scar.

By then, the Covid pandemic had begun, so getting to medical appointments was challenging. , Our household took extra precautions because Max didn't do well with even a minor cold, so I thought Covid would threaten his life. We stayed home. We got vaccinated. We followed all the rules.

And I had cancer, clear cell renal cell carcinoma (CCRCC). Luckily the margins of the mass were clean, and it was at stage 1, grade 2. With that diagnosis, I had the best-case scenario but it shook me to my core. I thought I'd die waiting for the final test results and surgery. I felt I was losing my mind, and started writing.

I was given long-term disability, but I was released after surgery, I couldn't bring myself to go back to work. I started seeing my family doctor again. At forty-eight-years-old, I finally admitted that uncontrollable depression was slowly killing me.

Umpteen tests and consultations with psychiatrists and psychologists confirmed a diagnosis of depression, anxiety, bipolar II disorder and PTSD. It was on paper, in black and white. I had the same illnesses that took the lives of my brother, my mother and my husband. I'd witnessed it all and decided to act differently. I decided to obey the doctors, who prescribed anti-depressants, anti-anxiety, and other medications to balance the chemicals in my brain.

While they experimented with dosages and medications, I lost my van and had to sell my furniture to pay the mortgage. My 401(k) shrank until it disappeared. Every day, I woke up asking how I got there and cried in the shower with the water running so Max wouldn't hear.

The question wasn't how I got here. The better question was how do I get out?

There was no single turning point, no magical moment when it clicked and I chose healing. Slowly, reluctantly, I crawled out of the wreckage. The medications stabilized me and I felt well enough to take a part-time job and accept help from my sister Amie.

We moved into a small house on Charlotte Mill. I began homeschooling Max, not because I wanted to, but because it was the only way to protect him from illness. He'd remained healthy during Covid, so after the quarantine lifted, I opted to continue virtual classroom instruction with the support of the school system. He did, and still does, classroom activities, physical, occupational and speech therapies from home.

Every morning, I got up, made coffee, opened my laptop, and began building a life again — one invoice, one email, one therapy appointment at a time. I've learned that healing doesn't begin with motivation but with brutal honesty, with asking yourself what isn't working and being willing to burn it down.

I'm no longer the little girl in the red coat or the teenager crying herself to sleep over a mother who can't stay sober. I'm not the young woman trying to earn love by being useful. I'm neither a martyr nor a victim, nor even a survivor.

I'm a builder. A breaker of cycles. A mother. A writer. A damn good accountant.

And I'm still here.

Staying alive might be my most radical accomplishment — not just breathing but *living*. Choosing to tell the truth, even when it shakes the ground beneath me. Choosing to raise my children in clarity, not confusion. Choosing to finally, fully, be myself.

This is the final entry in the diary of a Dog Patcher — the one where I come home to me. The one where I stop asking how I got here and start deciding where I'm going.

CHAPTER SEVENTEEN

Legacy

What is a legacy?

I used to think it meant money. Land. A family name. Something you leave behind, written in a will or engraved on a tombstone. But I've come to understand that legacy is less about what we leave and more about what we carry forward — and what we choose not to carry at all.

For generations, my family carried silence. We carried shame. We carried grief like an heirloom passed from one broken heart to the next. We buried secrets. We drank down our pain and never called it by name. We survived — but we didn't heal.

Until now.

This book is my reckoning. My resistance. My repair. It's the story of what happened, yes. But it's also the story of what I refused to let continue, and what I chose to unlearn so my children wouldn't have to carry the weight I was born into.

Ciera, Max — this is for you.

I want you to know that trauma is not your inheritance. You're allowed to live a soft, peaceful, safe life. You're allowed to take up space, to feel your feelings, to speak your truth without fear. You're allowed to choose partners who are kind. Friends who are gentle. Joy that doesn't cost you your dignity.

You come from warriors and survivors, but you are not required to carry their battles. You are allowed to rest. To laugh. To thrive. That's your birthright.

If I leave anything behind, let it be this: a trail of truth through the forest of silence.

Let it be this book — A map, a mirror, a love letter.

Let it be me, choosing to live honestly. Choosing to love loudly. Choosing to end the cycle with me.

That is my legacy.

And I give it to you freely, with a heart wide open and a hope that you never have to fracture yourself to feel whole.